Wanda Wolosky

After All:
Life Can be Beautiful

After All:
Life Can be Beautiful

By Wanda Wolosky

To contact the author or order
additional copies of this book
afterallvarda@gmail.com

This edition was prepared for printing by
Ghost River Images
5350 East Fourth Street
Tucson, Arizona 85711
www.ghostriverimages.com

Cover design by the author

ISBN: 9780692103234

Library of Congress Control Number: 2018904135

Printed in the United States of America

Revised Second Edition: July, 2018

Contents

Foreword.. IX

Prologue.. XV

Ancient Wars... 1

World War I.. 5

World War II... 11

Early Childhood Memories 19

The War 27

On the Aryan Side and The Warsaw Ghetto Rising 39

The Polish Uprising and Russian Liberation 49

Israel 65

To the United States, Israel and Back to U.S. 77

My Mother's Story... 91

The History of the Warsaw Ghetto 103

Letters from Students and Faculty-Part 1........................ 127

Letters – Part 2... 169

Afterword: The Fight For Statehood.............................. 185

After All: 193

Acknowledgements... 194

Works Cited... 195

My mother

This book is dedicated in memory of my mamusia
(mother) and my husband Gerry.
To my children and grandchildren–
Remember your heritage.

My husband Gerry

Foreword

Miracles sometimes occur amidst madness, mayhem and mass murder. As a small child, Wanda Wolosky smuggled food into the Warsaw Ghetto. Her acts of defiance document the enormity of her spirit in the body of a starving little girl. She and her mother managed to outlast the Holocaust, to make their way with a remnant of their fellow survivors first to Israel, and then to the United States. Wanda's mother lived more than nine decades, long enough to enjoy grandchildren and great grandchildren, long enough to enjoy the sanctuary that this nation has offered so many millions of the oppressed. Wanda is no longer that frightened-but-determined little girl, but neither has she forgotten the past.

Wanda has devoted much of her life to serving as a witness to history. her own heroes include those defiant Jews who persisted in conducting classes for children in the camps, who preserved Jewish rituals despite Nazi depravity and the world's indifference, those who died fighting disease, starvation, torture, slave labor and genocide, and those who fought back. Wanda's heroes include those Jews who resisted in myriad ways, escaping camps, foraging in the forests, fighting as partisans and with resistance movements and staging ghetto revolts that took longer for the Nazi hordes to suppress than whole nation states that succumbed precipitously in the wake of Nazi assaults. Wanda's heroes include those Righteous Gentiles who risked death to defend Jews. Many were hidden or helped in various ways despite the savage retaliation the fascists and their collaborating apprentices unleashed upon them. Wanda also includes the American military whose sacrifices made possible the eventual liberation of the camps, unconditional surrender of the Axis Powers and the survival of those Jews who had not yet been victimized by "the Final Solution."

Wanda is one of a group of Holocaust Survivors who meet in Tucson not simply to remember, but to reach out. They are the members of a Greek Chorus dedicated to retelling the tragedy of the Holocaust. They are the transcendent tribe committed to answering those who deny the truth. They are the courageous contingent of teachers who travel around the nation from schools to military bases to police departments to virtually any forum that will permit them to pass down their personal legacy. They were enveloped in evil. They survived. They fan the flames of memory and stamp out the flames of hatred. They are the guardians of what is possible when people forget the lessons of humanity.

On Sunday, February 8, 2009, Wanda Wolosky, Warsaw Ghetto survivor, introduced a poignant program entitled "Remembrance and Reflections on the Holocaust: A Tribute to Heroism and Freedom – Yom Hashoah Commemoration." From the opening presentation of the colors by American Legion Post #66 to pianist Michael Gervan's stirring arrangement of "Exodus," from the procession of the survivors escorted by students from the Billy Land Lauffer Middle School of Tucson to the unveiling of a plaque dedicated to the memory of the six million Jews, to the Invocation by Rabbi Louchheim of Congregation Or Chadash, the program was powerful. From the songs of the partisans and the sorrowful adieu to butterflies that were never again seen within the walls of the ghettoes all performed by the Tucson Jewish Youth Choir directed by Cantor Janece Cohen and Karla Ember to the haunting performan of "Ani Ma'amin" by Sara Golan-Mussman, from the candle lighting ceremony for the six million, for five million other victims slaughtered by the agents of savagery, for the Righteous Gentiles and for the Liberators, from the poems commemorating the best and worst of human words and deeds, from the plaintive violin of Diana Olivares playing the tune from Schindler's List (movie) to the poems and stories recounted by survivors, from Cantor Cohen's singing of "El Malei Rachamin" to Rabbi Louchheim's recitation of the Mourners' Kaddish to the blowing of the Shofar by Daniel Cancino there were words and music that struck a note of defiance in the face of despair. Michael Mussman delivered the Benediction, Wanda made a few brief closing remarks and the audience sang "God Bless America" and "Hatikvah" being led by Rodney Glassman (council member) and accompanied by Ladelle Peabody. There was a recession of survivors and retreat of the colors that unite us all. Father Rick Zamora of Salpointe High School established the ongoing relevance of remembrance in his timely remarks. He acknowledged the fact that all of us who know about the Holocaust are obligated to extirpate anti-Semitism from our institutions and our hearts. Cathy Simon of Desert Christian High School participated in the candle lighting. It was Ms. Simon who directed the magnificent production of "Fiddler on the Roof" by 80 students of Desert Christian High School last November that benefitted the Holocaust

Survivors. Yet another distinguished participant in the candle lighting was Dalles Peyton, of the 20th Armored Division, liberator of Dachau. As a member of the U.S. military, he continued the tradition of warrior liberators. To the exhibit of coins and medallions of the Holocaust displayed by Severin Szperling. By the time the program ended, the audience had truely become participants, sharing in the shock of the statistics of death, in the tears of empathy, and in the joy that so many fought back and continue to fight back. By telling the story of the Holocaust, one victim, one survivor at a time, Wanda is keeping faith with both the living and the dead. How fitting that Wanda's introduction to the Holocaust was the time of her childhood and that her program was attended by an intergenerational outpouring of support. One and a half million Jewish children under the age of twelve were slaughtered. Wanda Wolosky survived. For that miracle and for the miracle of all the children in the audience and in the program, and for the miracle of all the generations that issued from the survivors, we are all grateful.

Len and Dana Willens
Beth Shalom Temple Center
Green Valley, Arizona

• • •

Soldiers of the 45th Infantry Division were the first to arrive at Dachau

Two divisions of the US Seventh Army were involved in the liberation of the Dachau main camp on April 29, 1945, and with each passing year the argument grows more heated over which division really liberated the camp, the 42nd Infantry Division or the 45th Infantry Division. The 20th Armored Division was providing support and they are included as liberators of Dachau by the US Army. However, Japanese and African-American veterans have also made claims that their divisions or battalions liberated Dachau.

• • •

The following poem was written by Jaden Espinoza when she was a student at Billy Land Lauffer Middle School:

Dachau Liberators

Oh, Liberators the terrible smells you had to face
Walking through those camps not sure of what to expect
You see that the outside doesn't look like such a bad place
Until you walk in and see the boxcars full of bodies that you have to inspect

Oh, Liberators the sight of such deceitful signs
That lured the victims straight into their own death
Without Infantry Division 45 the Jewish population would not be fine
They are now growing, re-populated, and ready to thrive

Oh, Liberators what a hero you are too many
Your legacy will live on and on
Knowing that you had saved plenty
Making what you went through all worth it

Dear Wanda,
Mrs. Lydia Castillo told me that you wanted a little history of why my students wrote the poems that they did.
During the 3rd quarter, our curriculum is the study of the Holocaust with the overriding theme of "Finding Light through the Darkness" and "Can one person make a difference." I change the curriculum to fit my needs and here is how I change it: I have identified three groups of people during the Holocaust - Survivors, Resistors, and Liberators. I then divide the students into three groups and give them articles on Survivors - which also include Jehovah's Witnesses, and Gypsies. The Resistors get individuals such as Hannah Sennesh, and the Bielski Brothers to name a few. The Liberators are all American soldiers who helped liberate the camps and made sure that what they saw was not forgotten. After the students have studied the background of the individuals they are studying, they also study their role in WWII. How they survived, resisted and liberated. After all studying is done, the students then take all of that information and

create a movie that depicts the life and times of the individual they studied. In addition, students add pieces of art, poetry and visuals to their movie.

The next step in the process is to have the students study Odes. After they are comfortable with what an Ode is, a tribute to a person, they then write an Ode on the person that they studied, hence the poems that you received.

I hope this helps and I want to again express my thanks for speaking with our students and making my students "Famous!" They are thrilled that you are using their poetry.

Sincerely,
Lyslie Ijams
Lauffer Middle School

Prologue

You may ask why it is that I now have a burning desire to tell the story of my horrendous childhood as a victim of the Holocaust. For years I was asked to write my story, but I was not ready. I took an imaginary box and put my painful past inside it, then closed the box and put it up high on an imaginary shelf. One's instinct is to try to forget the horrors of the past, but the Holocaust does not let you forget. It haunts you. I have come to realize, though, that in order to live a normal life, I have to summon the strength and courage to look back.

I never mentioned my past to my two children. From time to time, my mother would mention the past to them. I felt, though, that they should not have to carry the burden of my past. I believe my decision was correct. My daughter, Sharon, who only heard my story within the past few years, is a successful woman who worked as the Budget Officer at the U.S. Army Center of Excellence at Fort Huachuca, Arizona and is now the Assistant Chief of Staff, G4/8 Director, for the U.S. Army Recruiting Command at Fort Knox, Kentucky. Sharon is married to a wonderful man named Paul, who I love dearly. Paul served as a Major in the Army and is now a computer scientist for Information Security Engineering Command, Department of the Army, at Fort Huachuca. They have three children: Chance, Jade and Lin. My son Jessie is also a very successful man who has accomplished every goal he set for himself. To this day, Jessie has not heard the story of my past. My children have grown into decent human beings and productive citizens, and I am so very proud of them. I hope my grandchildren will follow in their parents' and grandparents' footsteps, and make us all even prouder.

Gerry

Discharge

I started to write my book in 2012. My husband Gerry became very sick in December of that year. When he got sick, we went to the VA hospital where he was in isolation for 10 days because they didn't know what was wrong with him. After being in the hospital almost a month, and just when we were ready to depart, a doctor came into his room to casually announce, almost as an afterthought, "By the way, you have cancer in your liver and lungs. If you go through chemotherapy, you'll live a year. Without chemo you have six months." This is how some of the doctors at the VA treated their patients.

After we left the hospital, with Gerry getting worse, I found a place where he could be treated properly. The VA did not help. At the end of January, 2013, Gerry passed away at 3:30 in the morning. At 4:30, I decided to go home. When I got to the house, everything was dark, despite the fact that we had lights that came on automatically from dusk to dawn. Coincidence?

Gerry's casket with the American flag

The Masons from the Masonic Lodge in Green Valley giving tribute to their dead brother

I wanted to finish the book quickly, and so I wasn't able to share with my readers everything that was on my mind. I sent the manuscript to the publisher and it came back on March 1, the day of my and Gerry's wedding anniversary. That year we would have been married 55 years.

Since then I've had more time to put more history and personal observations into the manuscript for a second edition, and want to begin that with a little history of Gerry, my husband.

Gerry, who was born in Brooklyn, New York, (and whom I loved dearly), was a big supporter of Israel. When he attended George Westinghouse Vocational High School in New York City (where he finished coursework in Optical Mechanics), he was collecting money to purchase guns to be sent to Israel. He was proud to volunteer to serve in the U.S. Air Force for four years. This was during the Korean war. He spent most of that time in Germany, where he was wounded in an accident that happened on the base. Something very heavy fell on his back.

In 1952, Gerry went to Israel for a visit, where he saw me siting in a café. I didn't notice him or pay any attention to him at that time, but when I came to the U.S. and met Gerry we were amazed at the coincidence. Also in 1952, Gerry went to the kibbutz

"Sde Boker," where he met David Ben-Gurion and donated money to the new kibbutz. He'd gone there to attend the wedding of a friend he'd served with in Germany, Eddie Driben, a Jewish cowboy from Montana who'd decided to immigrate to Israel. They were best friends. David Ben-Gurion was Eddie's best man and Paula Ben-Gurion was the bridesmaid. Eddie eventually became the head of security at Kiriat Arba, a commune in Hebron.

Gerry was very proud of his service, and I am also proud of his service because I understand what it means to serve your country. Gerry belonged to the Ancient Free and Accepted Masons—AF& AM—for over 50 years at the Level Lodge # 32 of the Masonic Fraternity of Connecticut. He was also a 32nd degree Master Mason. Masons are the oldest fraternal organization in the world, and were started by King Solomon when he built the temple in Jerusalem.

I am proud to be a Jew, but I am not a religious person. I find it hard to believe in a God that closed his eyes to the horrors of what one man can do to another man. I sometimes even now believe that God is on a long, long vacation because inhuman events continue to occur all around us. Judaism means much more to me than faith and observance of the religion.

There are many books and stories about the Holocaust, but each is different. They do, however, all follow a common thread: the suffering of the Jews, and others, at the hands of the Nazis and their many collaborators from other countries.

When I moved to Arizona I heard about a group of Holocaust survivors who met in Tucson. I went to a few meetings, but after a while I did not want to be involved. Then one day Gail Wallen, PhD, a historian and a chaplain who was the leader of the survivors group, met my daughter and inquired as to why I was not interested in being part of the group. Sharon spoke to me about the group and convinced me to give it another try. As I went back, Sharon and Gail encouraged me to begin to share my story.

The first time I told my story publicly was in 2005. I have since traveled to many military bases, universities and Jewish temples in the United States telling the nightmare of my past, sharing a common history that must not be forgotten. The group of survivors that I belong to is getting smaller as people pass away, some from old age and others from illnesses that were consequences of their past lives. Those of us that remain share a common history.

I am asked to speak at many schools to tell students the story of my past. I have received hundreds of letters from students who have heard me speak. I read every one of their letters, so I know that their lives have changed since hearing my story. I think how lucky those students are, with no worries and few responsibilities. We, the children of the Holocaust, didn't have the luxury of a childhood. We were forced to become adults overnight, fighting for survival, from the very start of the war. I truly believe that by sharing my life story with students, I am providing them with a different perspective on life—and history—that is essential to their growth and their future.

I will never be able to make up the six years I lost during the war, and I sometimes wonder if the students realize how good their lives are. To live in a country where you can say whatever you want, to live with the feelings of freedom, these are the most precious gifts a human being could ask for. There are so many others who have so much less. I want them to understand that they live in a country where they can make decisions about their lives and their futures, about what makes them happy. I want them to know how lucky they are that they can speak up when they feel something is wrong, and that they shouldn't wait for someone else to do it for them. Life is too sacred to simply throw away on a whim when things do not go your way. I want these students, and all the people I talk to, to be grateful for what they have.

When I was five years old, I stood up to a bully and I was not afraid. I always tried to be helpful to anybody who needed it. I would like to instill those same principles in the people I speak to. Don't make fun of people who look different or speak differently. Help them, and help defeat injustice.

As I have gotten older I have mellowed. My hatred toward those who stole my childhood has disappeared. I do not hate the Germans, or the Poles, or anyone else. I believe that hatred is self-destructive. Perhaps new generations will understand that all people are created equal, and that no one religion is better than another. Maybe one day the killing will stop and voices will finally shout, "enough is enough." Our planet is beautiful and we must not destroy it or each other.

Martin Niemoller, a German Lutheran pastor during World War II, wrote:

First they came for the socialists,
and I didn't speak out because I wasn't a socialist.

Then they came for the trade unionists,
and I didn't speak out because I wasn't a trade unionist.

Then they came for the Jews,
and I didn't speak out because I wasn't a Jew.

Then they came for me,
and there was no one left to speak for me.

Through The Eyes Of A Ghetto Child

I walk through the streets of the
Ghetto and see the destruction.
Children, skin and bones lying on
sidewalks dying.
Was this going to be my end **too**?
I'm only a little child.
No, I'm lucky, I have a mother
She will protect me.
Will she be able **when** it gets **worse**?
Will I be one of them **lying** in the gutter?
Will I survive and see a better day?
Everything depends if our luck held up.
No one will help.
No one cares if we live or **die**.
What will happen to us all?
Perhaps tomorrow will be a better day.
Perhaps tomorrow the sun will shine.
There has to be hope for a better day
and the nightmare will be over.

(Why after so many years are
the dreams coming to haunt me.
I awake drenched in sweat a cry
stuck in my throat. Three o'clock,
Another nightmare. I'm no more
than a little girl.
The war is over a long time ago.
Why is the past haunting me.)

-- Wanda Wolosky

Story to Tell

Throughout eternity
Throughout time
There have been few
That truly shine
I don't speak of rulers
Presidents, Queens, or Kings
I don't speak of the popular
With riches and all manner of things
The few of which I speak
Are not worshiped or praised
They aren't put onto thrones
And high into the air raised
They are those who lived
Through a time of hell
They are those who live
With their story to tell
They appear as average people
With wants and fears
Beliefs and doubts
Smiles and tears
But as you look deeper
Average is not what you'll see
What you see is different
What could it be
Eyes of understanding

A knowing heart
A sense of great strength
As they prepare to start
One after the other
They stand tall and proud
With solemn faces
Look out upon the crowd
Sadness fills their eyes
As they begin their story
They speak of the horrendous happenings
And then of longed for victory
They relieve the horror
Every time they recount their tale
They tell all willing to listen
To help the world prevail
To help ensure
The atrocities done
Are known by the masses
And are never again redone
The strength it took to survive
Is simply amazing at best
And their hope and faith
Was surely stronger than the rest
They are those who lived
Through a time of hell
And are heroes more every day
Because of the stories that they tell

This poem was written for me and two other Holocaust survivors by Randall Vonk in 2008 or 2009 after we spoke to US Air Force airmen at Goodfellow Air Force Base, San Angelo, Texas. At the time, Randall was an Airman First Class.

After All

Ancient Wars

My name is Wanda Wolosky, and I am a Holocaust survivor. I have to tell you my story in the name of the millions of people who were silenced forever in the Holocaust.

I am Jewish, so I am going to start my story in ancient Israel. Egyptian records carved in stone in 1209 BCE are the earliest surviving references to the Kingdom of Israelites. Even before that time, there had been many wars in the land that, according to the Old Testament (the Bible used by Jews and Christians), God promised the land of Israel to Moses.

During its long history, Jerusalem, the capital city of the Israelite Kingdom and what should be the current capital of the State of Israel, has been destroyed twice, besieged 23 times, attacked 52 times, and captured and recaptured 44 times.

In the year 70 CE, the Romans captured and destroyed the Jerusalem Temple, which was the center of the political, economic, and religious life of the Judeans, or Jews. The Romans then leveled Jerusalem and banned Jews from it.

Masada, Herod's royal fortress atop an isolated rock plateau situated at the Dead Sea Valley, became the last Jewish outpost. It was considered to be invincible, but in 73 CE, the Roman governor Flavius Silva marched against Masada with the Tenth Legion, auxiliary units and thousands of Jewish prisoners-of-war (to do the Romans' dirty work) and to help in the destruction of Masada.

The Romans decided to make an example of Masada to show that they would spare no expense and time to destroy any revolt anywhere in their empire. Josephus, a Jew but also a full Roman citizen, writes that the Romans built an enormous earthen ramp and a huge siege machine which they then pushed up the ramp under a barrage of rocks and arrows being fired from above by the Jews. A year later, in the spring of 74 CE, they finally broke through the walls of Masada.

When the 960 men women and children of Masada realized their defenses would soon be destroyed, they committed mass suicide rather than become Roman slaves. Only two women and five children survived to tell the story. Still not satisfied, the Romans changed the name of Jerusalem to Aelia Capitolina. They also changed the name of the country from Yehuda (Judah) to Syria Palaestina, (Philistine or Palestine Syria.) They did this to emphasize that the rebellious Jewish nation had lost its right to its homeland. The Jews, however, did not agree that they lost their right to their homeland as punishment for their revolt against Rome.

For the next 1,800 years, Jews mourned the loss of Israel and Jerusalem in song and prayer. Following the Roman wars, the Roman government forcibly deported many Jews from the Land of Israel. Many other Jews left their devastated country as refugees. Some of the exiles returned to the homeland, and many Jews stayed for generations in the land. (Beginning in the 1880s, Jews across Europe began collecting money to buy land in Palestine from the Turkish government and from large Arab landowners. They were purchasing regions that were sandy or swampy, infested with mosquitoes and with malaria. (Because of all the pogroms against Jews, and later the Arthur Dreyfus trial, Jews agreed that, without a country, they had no name, voice, rights or any way to enter into the fellowship of peoples.) But many of those who did not return wandered all over the known world, trying to find safe harbor. My ancestors were among them. After fleeing the wars in ancient Israel, and after many centuries of wandering, my ancestors settled in Poland.

I only have information on my mother's side of the family, and only from 1821. Because they were living in small towns most of the time, there are no existing records. Only in the 19th century did they move to Warsaw, the capital of Poland.

Today, Masada is a shining example and symbol of courage. On its summit, Israeli Army recruits swear their oath of allegiance. «Masada will never fall again.»

The first massive influx of Jewish immigrants into Polish territories took place after 1098. The next wave of Jewish immigration came at the end of the 12th century. These Jews were primarily traders and merchants. They brought luxury goods, fine fabrics, jewelry, salt and spices. Some were money lenders. With time, they became tax collectors for the rulers of principalities.

Another massive Jewish settlement to Poland began in the 14th Century by invitation of King Casimir the Great (Kazimierz Wielki, 1330-1370), who extended to the Jews political protection from persecutions.

Poland was a world of wealthy nobles and impoverished serfs. The peasants were exploited mercilessly. Nobles employed Jews to collect taxes, as they were suited for the task and had the ability to administer and handle large amounts of money and were politically powerless and would never interfere in struggles between rulers and the ruled. For stability, the Jew always supported the ruler and the noble under whose protection he lived.

At the time, Europe was reeling from the Black Plague epidemic (or the Black Death) which killed 30 million people. Because the Jews were accused of causing the outbreak of the disease and spreading it, King Casimir issued a statute granting his subjects extensive privileges, protections and freedoms. By the end of the Middle Ages, Jews in no other European country had as many extensive privileges as those in the Kingdom of Poland. 18,000 Jews lived in more than 90 cities and towns across Poland.

But the 18th century saw the limitation and elimination of Jewish rights and privileges. In 1763, only 1,365 Jews were permitted to settle in Warsaw. It was only in 1799 that Jews were permitted to settle in Warsaw. Restrictions on where Jews could live went back and forth. Even with all the restrictions, many Jews became very rich. But the majority were very poor.

Persecution and pogroms continued through the centuries, and Jews were very often killed. Through the centuries, Polish Jews had become pioneers of industry and commerce. Even with a very small number of Jewish students being allowed to study in Polish schools and universities, they became accomplished as bankers, financiers, and builders of universities and railroads. They were publishers, composers, musicians, conductors of philharmonic orchestras, poets, writers, painters and artists. They were scientists, doctors, physicists, chemists, mathematicians, lawyers, construction and electrical engineers, presidents of museums, presidents of stock exchanges, creators of buildings for the Warsaw University of Technology, and more. From a total of 520 Nobel Prize winners, 120 were Jews. Jews served in the military, and many died in battle for the freedom of Poland.

On the eve of World War I, 337,000 Jews lived in Warsaw. Prior to the outbreak of World War II in 1939, that number had grown to 370,000. Through the centuries, there were both good and bad times. All this changed for the very worse on the day the Germans occupied Poland.

World War I

To understand World War II you must know something about World War I, which lasted from 1914 until 1918. Any educated European who has studied ancient history should have learned that war was futile, but mankind had learned nothing. After all the ancient wars—the Babylonians, Assyrians, Persians, Greeks, Romans, and all the other ancient powers that constantly made war amongst themselves—modern European powers were doing the same thing. Russia, France, and Great Britain aligned against Germany, the Ottoman Empire (Turkey) and Austria-Hungary. Greed for land, ambitions to control the seas, fear of each other's militaries, and jealousies between royal families tied Europe up in a complicated knot of treaties and alliances. By 1914, tensions were so high that the June 28th assassination of the Archduke of Austria-Hungary caused Austria-Hungary to declare war against Serbs, since it was a Serbian group who had killed the Archduke. In turn, this caused the Central Powers (including Germany and Austria-Hungary) and the Allies (Great Britain, France, and Russia) to declare war on each other, all of which started World War I.

The United States did not enter the war for another three years. Both the American president, Woodrow Wilson, and the American people were very reluctant to enter any European war. On May 7, 1915, a year after war had started in Europe, German submarines sank the Lusitania, an American passenger ship, with the loss of 120 American lives. Even then, the Americans hesitated. Greatly fearing the threat of American involvement in Europe, Germany's Foreign Minister, Alfred Zimmerman, attempted to provoke Mexico and Japan into attacking the United States with a promise of German assistance and a share in the spoils of war after their victory. Zimmerman's telegram to the German ambassador to Mexico was intercepted and decoded by the British and sent to the United States, which further swayed the Americans to action. Finally, after the sinking of the Lusitania and the Zimmerman Affair, President Wilson asked Congress for permission to go to war. On April 6, 1917, Congress officially declared war. Like many Americans at the time, President Wilson justified America's involvement in World War I as "an act of high principle and idealism . . . (and) . . . as a crusade to make the world safe for democracy."

If defeat was not imminent, neither was victory. The colossal forces across Europe and in Eurasia held a death grip on the continent, and appeared to have canceled each other out. Only the addition of significant new forces on one side or the other seemed likely to tip the scale. This first great war, World War I, took the lives of over 15 million people! 20 million more were wounded, both military and civilian, making it one of the deadliest conflicts in human history.

But even after this terrible war, the world was about to see something even more terrible: the Spanish Flu. World War I was not the cause of Spanish Flu, but close troop quarters and massive troop movements hastened the spread of the pandemic, which soon spread throughout the world. Current estimates suggest that between 50 and 100 million people worldwide were killed by the flu. The 1919 pandemic has been described as the greatest medical disaster in history, and may have killed more people than the 14th Century's Black Plague. World War I and its aftermath was so horrible that some called it the "war to end all wars." Surely, then, mankind would never again be so foolish as to start another world war. The victors met at the Paris Peace Conference in 1919. If mankind had learned nothing from the futility of ancient warfare, surely they would learn from the horrible aftermath of World War I and the pandemic flu it helped foster. However, nearly all the forces on the winning side of the war wanted only revenge, punishment, and land. President Wilson's idea of "Peace without Victory" was long forgotten. They could not see that this would only lead to more war.

Germany wasn't even invited to the Paris Peace Conference. For six months, Paris was effectively the center of a world government, as the victors bankrupted entire empires and created new nations. But the most dangerous result of the Paris Peace Conference was that German was declared guilty. Its military was weakened, and it was required to pay all the huge costs of the war to the victorious nations. This was the War Guilt Clause, written into the final Treaty of Versailles. Just as significant was the division of Germany's colonial empires (and those of its allies) in Africa, southwest Asia, and the Pacific, all taken away from Germany and divided up among the victorious allies. Even parts of Germany itself were given to Poland, Denmark, Belgium, and France. The German Sudetenland was given to Czechoslovakia, which became one of Adolf Hitler's first excuses for starting World War II. British Field-Marshal Earl Wavell, who participated at the Paris Peace Conference, said despondently of the events there: "After the war to end wars, they seem to have been pretty successful in Paris at making the Peace to end Peace."

The Balfour Declaration

This printing block was found in Canada 100 years after it was made. It was used to print the Balfour Declaration in English and Hebrew on wood. The numbers of prints created is unknown, but the wooden prints were hung in homes as excitement of having a future Jewish nation built.

On November 17, 1917, Britain's Foreign Secretary, Lord Arthur J. Balfour, transformed the Middle East forever when he sent his now famous letter, The Balfour Declaration, to Baron Walter Rothschild, a leader of the British Jewish community. It read in part:

"His Majesty's government views with favor the establishment in Palestine of a national home for the Jewish people, and will use their best endeavors to facilitate the achievement of this object, it being clearly understood that nothing shall be done which may prejudice the civil and religious rights of existing non-Jewish communities in Palestine or the rights and political status enjoyed by Jews in any other country."

Before the Balfour Declaration, a Jewish homeland was a small movement comprised of dreamers that even divided the Jews and was dismissed by Gentiles (non-Jewish people). After the Declaration, the Jewish national project enjoyed the support of the leading imperial power of the age, Britain. Though he could not have known it at the time, Lord Balfour had laid the foundations for the state of Israel and a conflict between Arabs and Jews that remains unresolved even today.

In that document the British government promised to aid in the establishment of a Jewish home in Palestine. A British Jew, Chaim Weizmann, played a key role in that declaration. He had been born in a small, poor village in Russia in 1874, but had studied hard and had become a professor of chemistry in England by the time World War I began. In 1907, ten years before the Balfour Declaration, Weizmann had visited Jerusalem. He was horrified to see the city living on charity and bribery. Jerusalem was then under Turkish occupation. He left the city and went back home to Manchester, England, with a renewed vision to see Jerusalem once again ruled by the Jewish people.

By 1915, Weizmann had discovered a cheaper, faster way to make acetone, a key component in explosives manufacturing, for the British military. Winston Churchill himself asked to meet with Weizmann at the British Admiralty (the navy), who was soon after named Director of the British Admiralty Laboratories. Discussions between Weizmann and Lord Balfour had started a decade before the war, and Weizmann played a crucial role in the Declaration. The Balfour Declaration represents the first time a world power—Great Britain—openly supported and recognized the need for a Jewish homeland. The Balfour Declaration became the first officially sanctioned step toward what would eventually become the Jewish state.

At the same time, as the British were negotiating their agreements with Weizmann and the Rothschilds, the British Government was negotiating with King Abdullah Saud, the Sharif of Mecca, who represented the Arab people. The British were attempting to get the Arab Bedouins, under King Saud, to revolt against the Muslim Ottoman Turks and to support the British in their war against Germany and Turkey. A British diplomat,

McMahon, exchanged a series of letters with King Abdullah in which the British pledged their support for an Arab national homeland. King Abdullah agreed to enter the war against the Turks and Britain supplied the Arabs with weapons. The Arab Revolt was led by a British officer, T.E. Lawrence, commonly known as "Lawrence of Arabia." At this period in Britain there were more Arabophiles than supporters of Jews, and the oil in the Mideast was critical for the war effort.

To achieve their goals, the British were not overly concerned about the contradictions proposed by the Balfour Agreement and the McMahon Agreement. Nor were the British overly concerned that both agreements would prove to be largely worthless diplomacy. The British, the French, and their allies in the war, were secretly negotiating a plan on how the two nations would divide the Middle East and Ottoman Turkish provinces following the expected defeat of Turkey. This secret negotiation became known as the "Sykes Picot Agreement," Sykes representing the British government and Picot representing the French government. This agreement was a pure example of colonialism for the two countries to control the Middle East, and most importantly, the massive deposits of oil. Of course, the Ottoman Turks had to be defeated first, and the "Agreements" with the Jews and the Arabs were needed to achieve this end.

It is a sad fact that Britain later betrayed the Jews in World War II, shamelessly backing away from the Balfour Declaration. The British even closed the borders of Palestine to all Jews just as the Holocaust was beginning in Europe! This betrayal condemned millions of Jews to death since they had nowhere to escape. No country was willing to let Jews cross their borders.

Chaim Weizmann worked many years to see the birth of Israel. Finally, as World War II drew to a close, Weizmann's work paid off for the Jews. Because of the Holocaust—and for other political and religious reasons—in November, 1947, the United Nations voted to establish both a Jewish and an Arab state in a partitioned Palestine. The Jews realized that this would be the only offer they would get, and despite it being far from what the original Partition Plan had promised, they agreed to the offer and opportunity for state-hood. The Arabs, on the other hand, rejected it. The new nation of Israel was born, and on May 14, 1948, David Ben-Gurion, the head of the Jewish Agency (a Jewish organization that would become the government of Israel), proclaimed the establishment of the State of Israel. U.S. President Harry S. Truman recognized the new nation that same day. Fittingly, Chaim Weizmann was Israel's first president, serving until his death in 1952.

25,000 Palestinian Jews volunteered to serve in the British Army during World War I, though it took Britain two years to establish Jewish battalions. After the war, when Britain took possession of Palestine and the Balfour Declaration had been established, Jewish hopes were raised that they would soon have a permanent home. This was, however, an ingenious plot to gain possession of Palestine, the crossroads of three continents. (Even during World War II, after much hesitation, Britain consented to establishing a "Jewish Brigade Group," out of which came many of Israel's future army generals.)

The British occupied (Mandate) Palestine for thirty years. During their occupation, they arrested many leaders, both Jews and Muslims. The minute the United Nations established the partition, British troops swept into Jewish settlements and confiscated large quantities of arms which, in turn, they turned over to Arabs, along with fortified buildings, leaving the new Jewish nation defenseless. In May 1948, five Arab countries attacked the newly proclaimed State of Israel.

World War II

The Earl was right: just one year after the end of World War I, Germany was ripe for someone with Hitler's fearful talents and hatreds. The country had been humiliated, its economy ruined by the War Guilt Clause and other measures forced upon it by the allied victors.

In July 1919, when Hitler joined the German Workers' Party, it only had seven members. Prior to this he'd tried to join the larger German Socialist Party, but they'd rejected him. Had he been accepted, it's likely he'd never have been a leader in that party. The German Workers' Party was in place from 1919 to 1920, when it became the National Socialist German Workers' Party (abbreviated as NSDA). In English, this was the Nazi Party. The Nazi Party lasted until 1945, when World War II ended.

The number of members in the Nazi party grew larger each year. One of the cardinal principles of the movement was anti-Semitism. As the party grew, violence against Jews increased. From Hitler's first-ever public speech as a member of the German Workers' Party, at a beer hall in Munich, his rise to total power was rapid. Concerning that speech, Hitler would write in his book *Mein Kampf* (*My Struggle*):

"I could speak! After thirty minutes the people in the small room were electrified and the enthusiasm was first expressed by the fact that my appeal to the self-sacrifice of those present led to the donation of three hundred marks."

Hitler had found his great talent for speaking, and he could see immediately that this power could easily bend the people to his will. In *Mein Kampf,* he also wrote of the lack of intelligence and sheepish docility of the masses of his own people. In his speeches, he blamed all of Germany's problems on the Jews and communism. His hypnotic speeches and simple messages, repeated over and over, appealed to the ignorant, desperate masses just as he knew they would.

Hitler's first attempt at seizing power in Germany was suppressed by the government. He was arrested, and on April 1, 1924, was sentenced to five years in Landsberg jail, where he lived a cushy life and wrote his manifesto, *Mein Kampf.* He was released just nine months later.

On January 30, 1933, Hitler was appointed Chancellor of the Reich by the President of Germany, Paul von Hindenburg. By March of that year, von Hindenburg would surrender total power to Hitler's Nazi party. When the elder von Hindenburg died the next year, Hitler immediately declared himself Fuhrer. Step by step, from 1919 until 1933, Adolf Hitler—a failed art school student—had become the Fuhrer of Germany.

Under Hitler's direction, on March 20, 1933, the Nazis began to establish camps. One of the first was Dachau, created at first to hold political prisoners of the Third Reich. Dachau eventually became a model concentration camp, and a training facility for SS guards who would man the various other camps. (Hitler got the idea of establishing camps from the British, who did this during the South-African war of 1899-1902).

Power had been given to Hitler freely; he hadn't needed to seize it. He acted quickly to secure that power, and spent the next five years furiously rearming the German military in secret. In July 1933, the legalization of mass sterilization became the law. This allowed the Nazis to eliminate the weak, insane, and other degenerates they deemed a drain to their power. At the same time, the entire existing structure of Jewish life in Germany collapsed. The persecution of the Jews began systematically almost as soon as Hitler came to power. This began when the Nazis created several anti-Jewish laws. They were introduced slowly at first, so the civilian population would not realize the extent of the Nazi party›s anti-Semitism. In the first year of Hitler›s power, public burnings of Jewish books were staged. The Jews were branded as an «Alien Race.» The racists declared that «No Jew could be German.» This affected their lives tremendously, since the vast majority of German Jews considered themselves to be German first. To the Nazis, it made no difference that Jews had contributed significantly to Germany's cultural and economic life, or that their loyalty to their country and fighting for Germany had been awarded with wartime medals.

On April 1, 1933, large-scale anti-Jewish boycotts and demonstrations took place against all German Jews. There were random attacks on Jews and Jewish businesses. Yellow stars were posted on Jewish businesses. Windows and doors were smeared with anti-Semitic and indecent cartoons. German police and courts no longer protected the Jews. The SA (Storm troopers) stood outside Jewish shops to discourage people from going inside. Kosher foods were banned, and a Department of Racial Hygiene was established. Each year under Nazi rule, actions against the Jews grew more drastic. In total, 400 laws and decrees were passed. Due to sharp reaction from abroad and fear of potential damage to the economy, this boycott of the Jews did not last long.

The term *Nichtarier* (non-Aryan) was adopted in Germany on April 7, 1933. This law allowed the Nazis to remove various professional Jews from their jobs, including lawyers, judges, public officials, artists, newspapermen and doctors. Jews were being pushed out of employment. During the so-called "Night of the Long Knives" in June of 1934, Hitler gave orders to the SS to murder dozens, perhaps hundreds of people he considered political enemies. One month later, he stood before the Reichstag and publicly declared that he and he alone had been the judge and jury during the killings. From then on, the SS was a much-feared organization in Germany. Hitler was now the law.

Two years later, on Sept. 15, 1935, Germany adopted the "Nuremberg Laws," a Nazi doctrine that provided precise definitions of what it meant to be a Jew (the laws included definitions of Jews by origin, religion, blood and family ties). The laws deprived Jews the rights of citizenship within the Reich. Intermarriage and sexual intercourse between Jews and non-Jews was branded as "defiling of the race," liable by punishment. Anti-Jewish policies were directed against converts, individuals of mixed parentage and assimilated Jews as well, even those persons who had not had ties with Judaism for two or three generations.

The world press reported the plight of the German Jews. In the summer of 1938, delegates from 32 countries met at the French resort of Evian. Franklin Roosevelt, who initiated the meeting, chose not to send even a low-level official to represent the United States at the conference. Instead, he sent a personal friend. During the nine-day conference, delegate after delegate rose to express sympathy for the refugees. But most countries, including the United States and Britain, offered excuses for not letting in more refugees. Even efforts by some Americans to rescue children failed: the Wagner-Rogers bill, an effort to admit 20,000 endangered Jewish refugee children, was voted down by the United States Senate not once, but twice, in 1939 and again in 1940. To Hitler, the message was clear: nobody wanted the Jews.

By 1938, Hitler was ready to take on the world. He first declared that he only intended to unify all German-speaking people. In March of 1938, he annexed Austria to the Reich, then demanded the liberation of German people in the Sudetenland, a region of Czechoslovakia. These actions were in direct violation of the Treaty of Versailles. The Prime Minister of Great Britain, Neville Chamberlain, flew to Germany to attempt a settlement. Hitler, Chamberlain, Daladier of France and Mussolini of Italy, met in Munich. In September 1938, eager to avoid war, Britain and France agreed that Hitler should have the Sudetenland of Czechoslovakia, with the promise from Hitler for no more aggression. Hitler assured those at the meeting that this was the extent of his ambitions for expansion. Chamberlain returned to England with a piece of paper signed by Hitler, and proclaiming "peace in our time."

The Czechs were not represented at the meeting and, realizing that no country would come to their aid, were forced to surrender the Sudetenland to Germany. Despite the assurances given by Hitler in the Treaty of Munich, six months later he marched into Czechoslovakia and occupied the entire country.

The Night of the Long Knives was a decisive turning point in Nazi policy. Conditions for Jews were now far worse than any that had occurred thus far in Germany. Already in 1938, the Nazis felt ready to attack Jews all across the country. It is thought that Goebbels, Hitler›s Chief of Propaganda, ordered what came to be called «Kristallnacht» (The Night of Broken Glass), a grave incident that occurred on Nov. 9 1938.

The parents of 17-year-old Herschel Grynszpan, (son of Polish-Jews), who resided in Paris, France, wrote to him to tell him what was happening to them. They told him that they were being deported from Germany to Poland and had been detained at the Polish border for days without any food.

On November 7, Grynszpan shot Ernst Von Rath, the Third Secretary of the German embassy. He died on November 9. Attempts were made to persuade the British government to use its influence with the German government to suspend imminent retaliation against German Jewry. Britain refused to be involved or associated with any support. This was the perfect opportunity for the Nazis to attack the Jews. Gangs of Nazis roamed through Jewish neighborhoods breaking windows. At least 30,000 Jews were arrested (8,000 in Austria) and sent to concentration camps. They destroyed 815 shops, 29 warehouses, 171 dwellings, and burned 191 synagogues, of which 76 were completely demolished. Jews were physically attacked, beaten, and several were either injured or killed. The Germans attempted to present the «Action» as a spontaneous protest on the part of the «Aryan» population. In fact, it was unleashed by Nazi leaders. They even blamed the Jews and had Jewish insurance claims sent to the German Treasury. The Nazis imposed a fine of one billion marks on the Jews, as the punishment for creating this situation.

These measures put German Jews in jeopardy, and only further aggravated their situation with the systematic deportations of thousands to extermination camps in 1939. Many historians regard Kristallnacht as a crucial turning point in Nazi policy regarding the Jews, and consider it to be the actual beginning of what is now called the Holocaust.

In May of 1939, a German ocean liner, the *MS St. Louis*, was moored in Hamburg with 937 German Jewish refugees aboard. The ship was to sail to Cuba where the refugees were promised freedom. Not only were they denied entry to Cuba, but also to the United States (due to the State Department's Anti-Semitic position, the U.S. did not look favorably on Jewish immigration) and Canada. The ship returned to Europe, docking at Antwerp, Belgium, on June 17, 1939. The United Kingdom agreed to take 288 of the passengers, who disembarked and traveled to the UK by other steamers.

After much negotiation by Gustav Schröder, the ship's captain, the remaining 619 passengers were allowed to disembark at Antwerp; 224 were accepted by France, 214 by Belgium, and 181 by the Netherlands. (They were safe from Hitler's persecution only until the German invasions of Belgium and France in May, 1940.) Responding to the shameful journey of the MS St. Louis, the German government was able to state with great pleasure how "astounding" it was that foreign countries criticized Germany for their treatment of the Jews, but none of them wanted to open their doors to them when "the opportunity was offered." Of the 620 passengers who returned to continental Europe, only 365 survived the war.

On August 23, 1939, Hitler's Germany and Stalin's Russia stunned the world by announcing that they had concluded a non-aggression pact, committing themselves not to aid each other's enemies or to engage in hostile acts against one another. Stalin knew the pact would not be popular. "For many years now," he said, "we have been pouring buckets of shit on each other's heads, and our propaganda boys could not do enough in that direction. And now, all of a sudden, are we to make our peoples believe that all is forgotten and forgiven? Things don't work that fast." The front garden of Nazi party headquarters in Munich was quickly filled with party badges and insignia thrown there by party members appalled at the thought of an alliance with the communist enemy they had spent their lives fighting against.

The shock would have been all the greater had people been aware of the secret clauses of the pact, with subsequent addenda, in which the two states agreed to partition Poland between them – Germany taking the larger part – while Hitler conceded that the independent Baltic states of Latvia, Lithuania and Estonia, Finland, and parts of Romania would fall into the Soviet sphere of influence. Just over a week later, On Sept. 1, 1939, Hitler invaded Poland from the west, his armies brushing aside the brave but ill-equipped Polish army. Britain and France, having signed a treaty with Poland, declared war on Germany. And thus the second world conflict of the 20th century begun. Shortly afterwards, the Red Army marched into the eastern part of Poland. In 1940, Stalin's troops marched into the Baltic states. His attack on Finland was initially repulsed in the "Winter War," but in the end and an uneasy peace was reached, marked by Soviet annexations of Finnish territory in the east of the country. Further south, the Soviets seized Bessarabia and northern Bukovina from the Romanians.

On March 5, 1940, thousands of Polish officers surrendered to the Red Army when the Russians invaded Poland from the east. The Polish officers were taken from the prison of Kozelek, which was a war camp, to the forest of Katyn in Russia and executed by the NKVD. Between 21,768 to 22,002 Poles were murdered. Of them, 8,000 were military officers, and 6,000 were police officers. All the others were priests, lawyers, landowners, factory owners, and members of the intelligentsia.

On June 22, 1941, Germany attacked the Soviet Union, breaking the treaty Hitler had made with Stalin. Stalin asked the United States and Britain to open a second front in Europe. The United States finally entered the war in late 1941 following a sneak attack by the Japanese at Pearl Harbor, Hawaii. The little known British field marshal, Earl Wavell, had been correct when he said that the Treaty of Versailles that ended WWI was not "the War to end War"; instead it was "the Peace to end Peace."

As early as 1933, at the start of Hitler's reign, the Third Reich established about 110 camps specifically designed to imprison some 10,000 political opponents and other "undesirables" and enemies of the state. As Germany invaded and began occupying its European neighbors, the use of camps and ghettos was expanded to confine and sometimes kill not only Jews but also homosexuals, Gypsies, Poles, Russians and many other ethnic groups in Eastern Europe. Ghettos were sections within cities where Jews had to live, and where Jews from smaller regions were sent. The camps and ghettos varied enormously in their mission, organization and size, depending on the needs of the Nazis. The numbers are astounding: 30,000 slave labor camps; 1,150 Jewish ghettos; 980 concentration camps; 1,000 prisoner-of-war camps; 500 brothels filled with sex slaves; and thousands of other camps used for euthanizing the elderly and infirm, performing forced abortions, "Germanizing" prisoners or transporting victims to killing centers. In Berlin alone, there were some 3,000 camps, while Hamburg held 1,300 sites.

The largest Nazi site identified for containing Jews was the infamous Warsaw Ghetto, which held about 500,000 people at one point.

Nazi Germany was admired by a large part of the Islamic world. One of the leaders in Mandate Palestine and the leader of Middle East Muslims was Hajj Amin al-Husseini, the Grand Mufti of Jerusalem and one of the most famous and respected Arab leaders of the time. He had been responsible for the Arab revolt in Palestine in the 1920s which caused a massacre of Jews in Hebron, as well as a second Arab revolt in 1939. He also was one of the biggest admirers and best friends of the Fuhrer, and a great admirer of the Greater German Reich. He admired how the Nazis were enacting genocide against the Jews. The Arabs were Germany›s natural friends (Arabs in Iraq, Syria, and Egypt had sided with Germany), because they shared common enemies with Germany: the English, the Jews, and the Communists.

The Mufti had visited Hitler a number of times. When he became a wanted man by the Brits in Palestine for criminal activities, he escaped to Berlin, where he remained for the duration of World War II. Husseini was not idle in Berlin: he made radio broadcasts to the Arab world exhorting his fellow Muslims to rebel against the British and to support fascist Italy and Nazi Germany. He also called for the massacre of Jews in Arab countries. An appeal by the Mufti to Arab countries produced a great number of volunteers eager to fight with fascist Italy and Nazi Germany. Husseini was also instrumental in helping to establish eastern European Waffen-SS divisions in countries such as Bosnia-Hercegovina and Muslims from Chechnya. For his help, he requested backing for Arab independence and support in opposing the establishment in Palestine of a Jewish national home. The Nazis promised the Mufti financial and other forms of support after war's end, a promise that Germany lived up to. When the independence of Israel was declared, the Great Mufti led the Palestinians in a war against the Jews with German advisors. The Mufti was aware of the Final Solution, and the plan to exterminate European Jews. He toured the camps with Himmler, and planned to kill the Jews in Arab countries and Palestine.

Early Childhood Memories

Uncle Henry, Grandmother Rose, and my father. My grandmother left for the United States in the 1930s. This is one of only three photos I have of my father.

I was born in a Jewish hospital on Czysta Street in Warsaw, Poland. I was named Gita, though I would change my first name several times throughout my life. My mother was Blima Szturman Milsztajn, and my father was Abram-Lejb Milsztajn. They married in 1932.

My earliest memories go back to when I was very young and my parents and I lived with my grandfather, Jakow Szturman, who was a tailor and was living in a rented shop. I was very close to my grandfather. I loved him more than anything, and he loved me. He took care of me. He sang to me in Yiddish, and I remember that he had a beautiful voice. He was religious and attended synagogue. Though my father was a "Kohane," my parents were not very religious. They attended synagogue on the High Holidays. They may have taken me as well, because throughout my younger years I remembered the melody of one specific song, the song of "Kol Nidre," a song that is sung on the most holy day of the year, "Yom Kippur," the day of atonement.

My first language was Polish, but when the adults were talking about something they did not want me to understand, they spoke in Yiddish (Yiddish is the language of Jews living in central and eastern Europe and is a mixture of German and words from whichever country you lived in, along with a little Hebrew. It was used daily, as Hebrew was considerd a holy language and was only used for prayers). They thought I didn't understand, but I did.

When grandfather was a young man he was supposed to serve in the Russian army. They would take Jews to serve for twenty-plus years. Most never came home. Grandfather had his little toe removed, so he did not have to serve. This saved his life.

Grandfather was born in the town of Tyszowce, in the southeastern part of Poland. The family was very poor, and lived in a hut that had a packed dirt floor. As I wrote in chapter three, I was able to trace the Szturman family back to 1821, though we cannot find records any earlier than this.

During the First World War, there was no work for my grandfather in Warsaw, so he decided to leave the city and take his family to his mother's home. His first wife passed away when my mother was young. Along the way, he was caught by the Germans. A German officer promised to let him go if he would agree to return to Warsaw. My mother had told me that during the First World War, once the Germans occupied Poland, German soldiers were kind and gave chocolate to children (quite a difference between World War I and World War II).

But my grandfather was determined to get to his mother's home, and contacted a Jewish group who loaned him a horse and wagon. In this way, he managed to get to his mother's home in Tyszowce. Because he was an excellent tailor, and from Warsaw, he got lots of work there.

My mother told me that she would cry every time her grandmother washed her hair. This was because she would use the same water that she had just cooked potatoes in to save coal.

When World War I ended in 1918, the family returned to Warsaw. Looking back now, it occurs to me that my mother was seven years old when that war began and eleven when it ended. I was five years old when World War II began and eleven years old when it ended. This fact has an emotional effect on me.

After World War I, my great aunt (my grandfather's sister), her husband, and the daughter of another great aunt, left Poland for Palestine. Thanks to the fact that they left Poland and had children and grandchildren, this is the only family I have.

My grandfather shared his shop with a woman who had a business making brassieres and girdles, and our entire family lived in the same space. The living area was divided from the shop by a curtain.

Before I was born, my mother had a baby boy who died soon after. She believed that perhaps this was for the best. She was young enough to have more children. So I was an only child. After being a widower for a long time, my grandfather married my grandmother's sister and had two sons with her. They were my uncles, Aron and Zeilik. There was also another uncle, Mordechai, who was married and had children. There were other relatives, but I don't remember them.

My father's brother, Heniek, was married to Zelda Wisniewski. His older sister was married and had two children. I don't remember their names.

I always loved animals, especially dogs, and I remember seeing a puppy and wanting one so that I could have something of my own, something that would belong only to me. My father told me I couldn't have a dog, which made me very mad. It was the only thing I'd ever wanted. When he asked me later to bring him a book, instead of handing the book to him I threw it at him. He put me over his knee, took off his belt, and gave me a beating, leaving belt marks all over my thighs. I used to wear short dresses, and everyone could see the evidence of the beating on my thighs. When I went out on the street other children asked me what had happened, I wasn't ashamed to tell them. I was very proud to have received that beating, because my father had also taught me a lesson. He pointed to the book and said, "You see that book? When you learn how to read you are going to find knowledge in books. You don't throw them, you cherish them." He was absolutely right. After I learned how to read, I never stopped. To this day, I can't go to sleep without first reading part of a book.

Whenever I saw a dog, I would run over to pet it. One time, when a big dog jumped up on me, my mother was sure it would scare me, but it didn't work. The next time I saw a dog I went right over to pet it, just as I'd always done.

My father was a very good-looking man. He had a gold tooth (the style at the time), and women were always chasing him, or he was chasing them. Who knows. But one day he left us. He was married to my mother, but he had another woman on the side. He visited us from time to time. Once, when I was still very young, he took me to show me off to some women. I don't remember where, or whom, exactly. It may have been his mother, my grandmother Rose Milsztajn, who was leaving for the United States. I do remember that I did not want to go, and I was crying because I was so mad at him. When we got

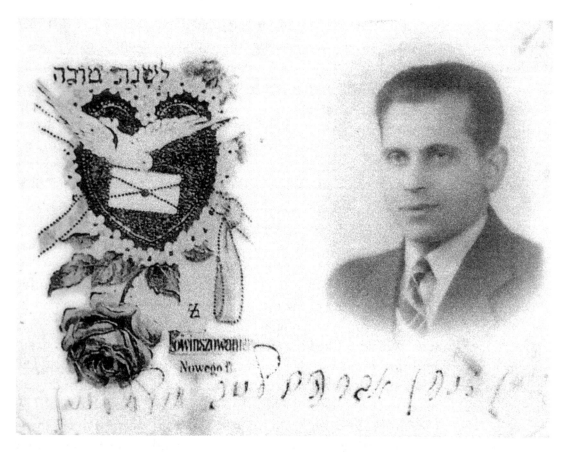

This photo of my father was sent to my grandmother in New York with a New Year's wish.

to the apartment, he pushed me into the room, and I peed all over the floor on purpose. This was my revenge for forcing me to do something I didn't want to do.

My father was a member of the Polish Bund, a Jewish Social Democratic Party that promoted the autonomy of Jewish workers and worked against antisemitism. He and a partner were butchers who opened a wholesale slaughter house in Praga, across the river from Warsaw. Praga is located on the east side of the river Vistula (Wisla). Since Warsaw was divided by the river, I didn't see him very often after the business opened.

We weren't wealthy. It was difficult to get work, so grandfather was doing alterations for people. I remember that he made me a coat. It was big, but it was pretty. It is the same as I am wearing in the picture.

My mother had graduated from high school and wanted to attend a vocational school.

She spoke Polish fluently, which was unusual for Jews in Poland, who mostly spoke Yiddish. One of her cousins was doing manicures and encouraged mother to learn the trade so she could go into business for herself. Mother like the idea, so she learned how to do manicures and pedicures. She was very good at her job, and she built up a good clientele. Most of her clients were wealthy non-Jews. She was really all on her own. It wasn't easy for her, because she was always working. She needed to make a living for us. She always took great pride in my appearance, and I was always dressed nicely. She also made sure I was always clean looking.

One of my fondest early memories was when I occasionally accompanied her to her work in clients' homes, giving them manicures and pedicures. She was very strict, and when she took me with her I would have to behave, sit in one place, and touch nothing. If I did something wrong, she would give me a look that could kill. Sometimes I received a good beating, but most of the time I deserved it. It wasn't because she didn't love me; it was because she did love me. It was a different time and there was a different attitude towards raising children. It wasn't out of the ordinary to spank a child, and I was always doing things I was not supposed to do. So my mother had her hands full with me.

I didn't have any toys because we didn't have money for toys. If I asked for something, mother would always say, "No, I cannot buy it. I can't afford it." Eventually, I stopped asking. We would walk by Pakulski Department Store and look at the electric puppets in the window. I could stay in front of the window and watch the puppets moving forever. I was so fascinated by them. I wished that I could sit and play with them. I knew mother couldn't afford to buy the toys, but I could still dream.

My mother always did whatever she could do for me, especially when it came to special kinds of food. Before the war in Poland they had watermelons which had been imported from Italy. There were peddlers on the street with carts who sold watermelon by the slice, and whenever we walked by them I would ask for a slice. I can still see the wagons full of those round watermelons. The thickness of the slice depended on how much money you could spend. To this day I can remember getting a slice, the dripping red juice so sweet. It was the same with oranges. Since my mother didn't have a lot of time for me, maybe that was her way of showing love. There was never any time for hugs and kisses; I had no idea what it meant to have a birthday. My birthday was just as ordinary as any other day. I never heard of birthday parties, or what it meant to receive birthday presents.

Once, my mother took me to see "Snow White and the Seven Dwarves." The only thing I remember is "Heigh ho, Heigh ho." I also saw a Shirley Temple movie, but I can't remember which one. I had a lot of respect for my mother and I loved her. I know that if she had not been with me through the war years, I would have never survived on my own. She was a very strong woman. She was very stubborn, and I was very stubborn too. When you put two stubborn people together, they will always clash. Luckily, those clashes occurred when I was older.

On Fridays, my grandmother made a large pot of chulent, a dish of meat, beans, barley and potatoes. We brought the pot to the local bakery, where it cooked in a brick oven for twenty-four hours. After grandfather left temple services on Saturday, he would take me to the bakery where we would pick up our meal for the Sabbath.

We lived in a section of Warsaw called Wola. We were the only two Jewish families on Staszyca Street. Everyone else on the street was Aryan. Everyone knew grandfather, and when an apartment became available – it was either 15 or 17 Staszyca Street – my mother and I moved there. It was across the street from grandfather's store. It was a ground floor apartment. I remember it was one room, with a kitchen in the back of the room and a window looking out on the street. There was no bathroom. When we needed one, there were toilets in the courtyard. Since we did not have a bathroom, the only way to get clean was a sponge bath each night, and when I got very dirty my mother scrubbed me so hard that I cried.

One of my saddest memories is of my grandfather dying of cancer in 1938. I remember the day very clearly. I was so devastated. I came into the room where he was lying on a bed, and mother told me that he had passed away, and that he was going to be buried. I threw myself on his body and started to cry. I didn't want him to go away. For a very long time, nobody was able to pull me off his body. I lost my defender, the one person who'd given me his unconditional love.

After grandfather died, my uncle Aron would sometimes take care of me. He was born in 1922, and I adored him. He was tall, maybe six feet, and he was good looking. He was a leader in the scouts, a huge Polish patriot, and belonged to one of the Jewish organizations. When he had time, he played with me and taught me games. He was like my big brother. I always wanted an older brother who could defend me and fight some of my battles. One day the family decided to put me in preschool. I hated that place. It was walled in and the gate was always closed. You couldn't get out, but sometimes I managed to sneak out. No one could figure out how. Ten minutes later I would be home. Of course I received a beating quite a few times. I was supposed to be at school, not at home.

There were only three Jewish children at the preschool. There was another girl, a boy, and me. All the others were Christians and they bullied us for being Jewish. They called us names like "Christ killer" and "Dirty Jew." Every time someone called me a "Dirty Jew," I would look at myself. I couldn't understand why they were calling me dirty. I was cleaner than some of them. I also didn't understand why they called me a "Christ killer." I didn't know who Christ was. How could I kill him? I was a small child. I didn't kill anybody. What was happening was that in the churches, the priests would preach, and in the schools the teachers would teach, that the Jews had killed Jesus. Nobody ever mentioned that Jesus was born and died a Jew. I didn't understand all of that. To this day, I still don't understand how it is that people can hate the Jews and at the same time pray to Jesus, who was born and died an Orthodox Jew.

The name calling happened all the time. There was only one seesaw in the preschool, and to use it, you had to wait your turn. One day, the other Jewish girl was waiting patiently for her turn to use the seesaw, but when her turn came a Polish boy went to her and pushed her. He said, "I'm going on the seesaw now, you Dirty Jew." Even though he was the biggest kid, and much stronger than me, I couldn't stand by and watch this injustice. I went over and punched him in the nose. He began to bleed and cry. I said, "She was waiting, and now you can wait." From that day forward, he was afraid of me, and stopped going after defenseless kids. I was kind of a tomboy. I wasn't afraid of anything. All my life I fought for underdogs. I learned very quickly not to show fear.

Sometimes I would play on the street with the other kids, games like Ring Around the Rosie, but not very often. I did not like to be called "Dirty Jew." Poland being a Catholic country and very anti-Semitic, treated Jews very badly. If a man or boy looked Semitic - dark skin, dark hair - and if he was walking alone, he would be attacked and beaten by Polish boys. My uncle Zeilik was born in 1925 and he spoke with a stutter. One day some Polish boys beat him up when he was coming home from school. The next day my uncle, Aron, was waiting for them. When the Polish boys saw Zeilik coming, they wanted to beat him up. But here came Aron. My uncles, together, beat the crap out of the Polish boys. From that day on, no one would fight with any of us on Staszyca Street. I learned this from my uncles and followed in their footsteps.

Each apartment house had a custodian who oversaw and took care of the building. My mother

My father and me. He sent this photo to his mother in New York. Taken in either 1938 or early 1939, this is the only photo I have of me as a child.

25

was very friendly with our building custodian and his wife. Sometimes they would look after me if I snuck out of the preschool, and occasionally they also took care of me after school. There was one woman who lived in our building who hated Jews, and hated us, but we didn't know why. "Oh the Jew woman," she would say all the time when she came face to face with my mother.

The War

Poland is situated in central Europe, between Germany to the West, Russia to the East, Czechoslovakia to the South and the Baltic Sea to the North. If you read Polish history, you learn that most of the time the country was occupied by her neighbors. Only after WWI did Poland become independent. It was not for long. On September 1, 1939, Germany attacked Poland. On September 28, the Warsaw garrison finally surrendered to a relentless German siege. On October 1, the victorious Nazi army entered Warsaw, signaling the persecution of the Jews and the decrees issued against them.

The Germans marched into my city. Before the war, almost 370,000 Jews lived in Warsaw, making it the largest Jewish community in Europe and second in the world after New York City. They comprised a third of Warsaw's total population, and 10% of Poland's population.

Most of them were very poor, living on assistance they received from American Jewish organizations. When Jozef Pilsudski was the leader of the Second Polish Republic, his policy was to respect all Polish minorities, whether they were Jews or Poles. He permitted Jewish students to join schools and universities. When Pilsudski died in 1935, everything changed for the worse. Only a limited number of Jewish students were allowed to enter universities. Riots against Jews become frequent.

Many Jews would have gladly left Poland for other countries, but no country was prepared to admit them. The British Mandate in Palestine closed its borders, as Britain objected to Jewish immigration to Palestine. Britain's indifference to what would happen to the Jews, whose survival depended on being allowed to enter Palestine, can be seen in the 1941 incident on the S.S. Struma.

The S.S. Struma was an old barge flying the neutral flag of Panama, and was chartered by Romanian Jews who feared what might happen to them once their transit visas expired. 769 of them boarded the Struma, which pulled into Istanbul on December 14, 1941. The old barge was in no condition to sail further, and the Brits still refused the Jews entry into Palestine. Because of this, Turkish officials refused to let the Jews disembark in Istanbul, and towed the Struma out into the Black Sea. It drifted there for three months, until it exploded. Only one of the Jewish refugees survived to tell the story.

The Evian Conference of 1938 applied only to refugees from Germany and Austria (for more on this, see the chapter called World War II). Of the 32 nations that attended the conference, only two accepted Jews.

One was Bolivia. Moritz Hochschild, a mining tycoon who migrated from Germany in 1881 to Bolivia, persuaded the Bolivian president to bring Jews there in order to help develop Bolivia's agriculture. He saved 9,000 German Jews, and is hailed as the "Bolivian Schindler" (Oscar Schindler save more then 1,200 Jews. His name was memorialized in the movie, " Schindler List").

The second country willing to accept Jews was the Dominican Republic, which offered to take in 100,000 refugees with funding conditions attached. In the end, only 854 immigrated to the Dominican Republic. But none of this was available to Polish Jews in 1939, and none of this much mattered to me: I was five years old, and my life would never be the same.

One day, my mother took me to work with her. There was a parade in the street. Polish cavalrymen with sabers were riding on big horses. My eyes were on the magnificent horses. My mother probably let go of my hand for a second, because I was almost under the hooves of the closest horse before somebody pulled me away. I had only wanted to pet the horse, but at the time I didn't know that these and other men were going to war on horseback against German tanks.

Of course, my mother knew about the war. It was in all the newspapers, though nobody discussed the war with me. I probably wouldn't have understood. My father and my uncle Henry, along with other men, decided to go to Russia. The Russians were not yet at war with Germany. In fact, they'd signed an agreement with the Germans to divide Poland between the two countries. I never got to say goodbye to my father, and I didn't even know he was leaving.

One morning I woke up, and I was all alone in the apartment. I heard planes flying overhead, and bombs falling. I went to the window and looked out onto the street. The street was a blanket of white down feathers that had come from pillows and blankets. A house was struck by a bomb. One house on the street was in ruins and another was on fire. I could see people in the street, running and screaming. The bombing continued day and night for a month and there was chaos in the city all this time.

The people started a volunteer patrol to make sure the gates to each apartment building were locked for safety. My mother took on these duties, and did so from 12:00-2:00 pm. She was a member of the patrol that guarded the gate to our building. They always had two people watching to make sure that when the siren went off, they could warn people to go to the basement.

There were bread lines at the bakeries. My mother was well known at the bakery across the street from our house, so she was able to get bread for a while. However, the bakeries soon ran out of flour, and starvation began to hit the city. The Germans had bombed the water pipes as well, so there was a shortage of water. I cried for days because I was so hungry. My mother could do nothing to ease my hunger. The German airplanes flew ceaselessly overhead. Even in the basement you could hear the sounds of the bombs hitting. If the hit was close, the basement shook. People were praying, hoping this was not their last day on earth.

After one month of fighting, the Polish army surrendered. Twenty percent of Warsaw was in ruins. Bomb craters were everywhere. People looked at the devastation and wept. The biggest area of destruction was in the Jewish section of Warsaw.

The Germans marched into Warsaw at the beginning of October, 1939, in trucks filled with soldiers, on motorcycles, but not too many horses. Everything was motorized. None of them smiled. The occupation had started. The occupiers immediately began to give decrees. They figured that all the people were dirty, so their first order was for everyone to be deloused. They sent groups of people to different locations for this. I went with my mother to the place we were assigned to. It was in a basement of a building. They told everyone to undress and then they sprayed us with DDT, which is a toxic substance that is no longer used because it is so hazardous. There were windows in the basement that looked out onto the street, and German soldiers gathered around the windows to gawk at the naked women and to joke and laugh at them. It was my first realization that these Germans were horrible people.

From this point on, try to put yourself in my shoes, see through my eyes, and feel what I felt. Perhaps you will be able to understand how life was for us. My life would never be the same.

The Germans decided that they were going to be nice, and were going to feed the starving people of Warsaw, but with one condition. "There will be no food for the Jews," they said. They supplied flour and told the bakery owners to begin baking bread, and told the people to form lines outside the stores. There were German soldiers standing guard, keeping the lines in order. If they noticed a man with a beard, or someone wearing different type of clothing, they would pull them out of line - by their beard if they had one - beat them up, telling them there was no food for Jews. My mother stood in line anyway (by the way, at times my memories of this period and my mother's don't always agree. For example, she recalls going straight to the front of the bread line). She picked me up and was holding me in her arms. Then it came our turn to get the bread. My mother got a loaf of bread, and the German soldier who was standing there turned around and gave me a loaf of bread too. This was unbelievable because no one was allowed to get more than one loaf of bread. Perhaps this was because of my blue eyes and blond hair.

As we were walking away with our two loaves of bread, a woman who lived in our apartment building who hated us because we were Jews was standing at the end of the line. She said, "Look at the Jew woman. She has two loaves of bread. By the time it's my turn, there probably won't be any bread left." So my mother took one of the loaves and said, "Here, this is for you," and gave it to her.

This woman couldn't believe that someone would do something like this, that a Jewish woman with a starving child would take a loaf of bread and give it to her. She stood there with her mouth open. This small act of sharing bread would later aid us in our survival. Unfortunately, that one loaf of bread we kept had to feed our whole family, not just my mother and myself but also one of my grandmothers and two uncles. We also needed to stand in line to get water.

The next act of the Germans was to put up posters advertising that they were looking for volunteers to work in Germany. So my uncle Aron said, "You know, they're looking for volunteers. I'm going to volunteer. I'm strong and I can work." I remember mother telling me that after a couple of months we got a letter from him saying, "I am working. Everything is Okay." A couple months later we got another letter, this time from the Germans, that said, "We're very sorry, but Aron got sick and passed away." Of course we had no idea what was going on so we believed it.

Now I question it. How could a six-foot-tall young man, healthy and with a good build, die like that in such a short time? But at that time we believed what the Germans told us. No one could believe that Germany, the most educated country in all of Europe, could come up with something like mass killing. No one wanted to believe it.

The Germans confiscated Jewish homes, furniture, household appliances, paintings, and valuables. If you tried to resist, they would punish you. They tortured babies, and beat pregnant women and the elderly. No one was safe at home or on the streets. Jewish women were publicly humiliated, forced to undress in the street and undergo body searches. The Germans took their jewelry and fur coats, and abused them sexually. If you tried to protest, you were beaten. They searched women's breasts and their private body parts, forcing husbands and children to watch. Fear was growing, and no one was sure what the next day would bring. No one was safe.

There were new orders all the time. Jews could only have 2,000 zloty in the bank, and could only withdraw 200 zloty per week to feed their families. I don't know what that was before the war, but in today's currency it's about five dollars to feed your family with. Another order came making it illegal for Jewish doctors to practice on Aryan patients. Teachers couldn't teach any more. If you had a business, you had to give it up. No work, no money, true starvation had begun.

Yet another order came down from the Germans. This time, they wanted the Jews who lived in different parts of the city to move into one section very close to the railroad tracks, in order to keep all Jews together. They told the Jews to move into designated areas, but each day the plan changed. If on one day a street was supposed to be in the designated Ghetto, the next day that would be canceled. Because of this, people became homeless.

My mother was lucky. She was able to exchange our apartment with an Aryan woman for her apartment in the Ghetto section on Nowolipki Street. She did this quickly; she did not want to wait until the last minute. The apartment was small, with only enough space to fit three single beds side-by-side, but that was fine. Grandmother was able to get a place for her and my uncle Zeilik in the same building. She was sharing her place with others. We were happy because we were close together. We did have some time to move some of our belongings, and we took whatever we could carry.

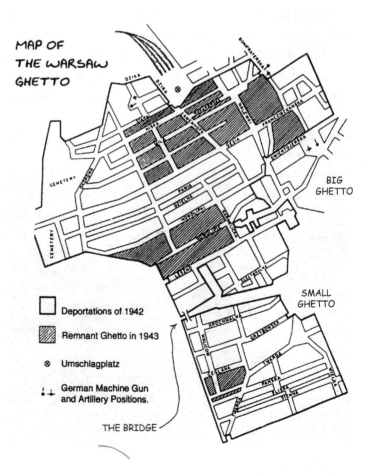

MAP OF THE WARSAW GHETTO

BIG GHETTO

SMALL GHETTO

☐ Deportations of 1942

▨ Remnant Ghetto in 1943

⊗ Umschlagplatz

↓↑ German Machine Gun and Artillery Positions.

THE BRIDGE

Soon after we moved to the Ghetto, many of the men who'd gone to Russia returned. One of them told my mother that the Germans had killed my father while he was near the city of Bialistok on his way back to Warsaw. She never told me this; I only learned of my father's death after the war.

You were not allowed to have American dollars, but we got a letter from father's mother, my grandmother Rose, who was living in the United States, saying that she was sending us money. In order to get our money, we had to leave the ghetto. There was a tram that went through the streets of the ghetto to the Polish side of Warsaw. Mother and I got dressed nicely and when the tram came through the ghetto, we jumped on it. Nobody said anything to us. Mother had to wear a white armband with a blue Star of David on it, but I didn't have to because this rule did not apply to children in Warsaw under the age of twelve. She took the armband off and put it in her pocket. We went to the bank, hoping all the way that we would be successful in getting the money out. When we got to the bank the teller stared at us but said nothing, and gave us our money. That was a miracle. We jumped on the tram and got off when we arrived back at the ghetto.

In March 1940, the Germans decided that it wasn't enough just to have all Jews in one section of the city. They decided that the Jews needed to build a wall around the ghetto, and that they had to pay for the bricks themselves. Jews took the bricks from bombed out buildings, cleaned them up, and began building the wall. The ghetto wall was 11.5 feet tall and included 13 gates. To prevent people from trying to climb over the wall, they put broken glass on top of it as an extra precaution. In some places, they put barbed wire.

Construction of the walls in 1940 by Jewish builders. Written on the Aryan sign on the walls, "typhus infected area", a warning to Poles not to enter the ghetto.

The ghetto's 13 gates were guarded by German soldiers, Polish police, and Jewish police. A Jewish committee, known as a *Judenrat*, was formed in the ghetto. They recruited Jews to serve as policemen to keep order in the ghetto and to perform other functions. Some of these Jewish police were not very nice. They figured that if they did something for

The ghetto wall. Height - 11.5 feet. Length - 11 miles

the Germans, they might get on their good side. It was like anywhere else. These Jews wanted power too. One of their jobs was to place as many people as possible in each room. But even so, there was not going to be enough room for nearly half a million people in an area designated for two hundred fifty thousand. A Jewish policeman was assigned to live with us in our apartment. He was a good guy, and provided us with some useful information.

Starvation quickly started inside the ghetto. It was the Jewish committee that organized the soup kitchens. You had to stand in line to get a slice of bread and watery soup with maybe a potato peel or two, but no real potatoes. If you didn't take the bread and quickly put it away, a child would grab it and stuff the entire piece in his mouth so you couldn't get it back. Or he would grab it from your hands, throw it in sewage water, pick it up and then eat it. You saw children walking around, looking like living skeletons. Some were laying on the sidewalks looking at you with big empty eyes. Their ragged clothes hung over their skeletal bodies. Some children wore shoes without stockings. They were skin and bones.

One of my mother's old clients owned a restaurant on the Aryan side, and her husband owned a brewery. We used to sneak out and work in the restaurant. Mother washed dishes, while I helped with whatever I could. When we worked we would bring food back for Grandmother and Zeilik. One time while we were working in the restaurant, I was throwing the garbage out, and a bee stung my leg. We didn't have access to medical care, and the sting became infected. It got bigger and bigger and filled with puss.

We couldn't go to any doctors, so I had to somehow take care of my leg on my own. Eventually it did get better.

In the Ghetto, I always went with my mother to some place that I don't remember to pick some items up from one place and take them to another. The only thing I do recall is that I was carrying very heavy items, and I know it was not food. I was never told what I was carrying. I only knew that my hands were painful for a long time after each of those trips, which we often made.

The food situation was getting worse and worse. My mother and I became smugglers. If you got caught smuggling you were shot on the spot. So, how were we able to get in and out of the ghetto? There were a few different methods for leaving the ghetto. Sometimes we went through cellars. Other times, when we heard rumors of a hole in the wall, we would get out that way. Occasionally we went out through the sewage system.

Many other times we would stand by the gate and wait for a good German to let us pass. Some of the Germans had a heart, but not too many. Polish winters were extremely cold, and we could wait for hours for a good German. I would shake, almost frozen, and cry from the cold and exhaustion. This experience left me with frostbite on two toes on each foot. Even today, I cannot wear anything with nylon because they burn my toes. Leaving the ghetto got harder all the time.

One day a Polish friend of ours came to see us. He was a foreman in one of the factories that had been established in the Ghetto. He had a pass that enabled him to come into the ghetto to work and to leave after work. He said to my mother: "Blima, I am going to take your daughter with me. She is going to sleep in my house and tomorrow I'm going to bring her back with food." That day he took me with him after work. I don't remember his name, and I don't remember exactly where his home was.

In the morning, he cut a big chunk of meat from the belly of a dead pig and wrapped it around my body under my arms. It was very tight under my coat, and I felt like I was in a cocoon. I walked with him back to the ghetto. The German guard at the gate asked him for his pass. After examining the pass and seeing that *"alles istin ordunung"* (everything was in order), the guard returned his papers to him. Then he looked at me, put his hand on my shoulder, and said in German, *"frierst du mein kin?"* (are you cold my child?) I was sweating from every pore of my body, because if his hand had touched just a little lower than my shoulder, he would have felt the meat that was wrapped around my body under my coat. Instead of hearing *"frierst du mein kin,* I would have had a bullet in my head. The food that I smuggled lasted quite some time.

One of my cousins was very rich. We visited him one day and he asked my mother, "Why are you going out all the time? One of these days they're going to catch you," to which she replied, "we don't want to starve to death." He asked, "Aren't you afraid of being shot?" My mother responded, "better a bullet than to starve to death." I remember when we visited him that he had food, but the only thing he gave us was a glass of tea and a cube of sugar. I thought, "why don't you give me a piece of bread instead of a lousy cup of tea, and don't lecture my mother what she ought to do."

Curfew was at seven at night. If you got caught on the street after curfew, you were shot. Not far from us was a prison by the name of Pawiak, where the Germans would take people they'd pulled off the streets or from their houses. If you wound up in Pawiak, you almost never came out alive. I know of only one person who ever survived Pawiak. Her name was Irena Sendler.

Irena Sendler was a Polish social worker who saved 2,500 children by smuggling them out of the ghetto. She wrote down the names of each child she smuggled out and put the names in a glass jar that she buried in her courtyard. Sendler joined an organization called ZOGOTA, the Council for aiding Jews in occupied Poland. This was an underground network founded in December 1942 by psychologist Adolf Berman and other prominent inteligentsia and social activists. One of their many tasks was to smuggle Jewish children out of the ghetto and provide them with false birth certificates and other relevant documents. Irena Sendler was a member of this secret organization.

Sendler was eventually caught by the Nazis, tortured by them to give the names of others in her organization (which she never did), and was supposed to be executed. The Polish underground bribed a German, and she was able to escape from Pawiak. She died when she was in her 90s. Because we lived so close to Pawiak, at night I could hear the shootings.

This scale model of the Warsaw Ghetto can be viewed by the public at Yad Mordechai Kibbutz in Israel

When any SS officer came into the ghetto, he was expected to have the entire sidewalk to himself. One day I was walking with my mother as an SS officer was walking on the other side of the street. There was a small child on the same side of the street as this SS officer who did not have enough time to get out of his way. The SS officer picked the child up by his feet and bashed his head against the wall then dropped the child's lifeless body in the gutter.

Rumor was that this was not the first time something like that had happened. Every day, if you didn't see it yourself, you still heard about it from others who'd seen all of these atrocities being afflicted upon the Jews. You would walk down the street and there were dead bodies lying all around. You stopped paying attention; it just became a daily occurrence. Tomorrow it could be you.

The smell of death was everywhere. A group of undertakers would pick up the dead bodies and throw them on a cart, and all of the dead bodies would then be thrown into a huge hole in the ground. Sometimes, a rabbi would say a quick prayer and that would be that. It would be time for the next group of bodies. Sometimes there were so many bodies lying dead in the streets that there wasn't enough time to pick them all up. They would lie there for a day, sometimes two. Some bodies were covered with newspapers. When someone died in an apartment, their body would be quickly put out on the street naked. In doing that, the clothes could be reused and no one had to pay for the funeral.

Sickness took hold of the ghetto. There was rampant malnutrition, tuberculosis, and typhus because of the lice, which were everywhere. They crawled all over everything, even the money that we used. It was impossible to get rid of them.

We got used to death in the ghetto streets. Walking past a dead body was just like walking past a live one. Life was cheap in the ghetto, of little value.

There was a big ghetto and a small ghetto. To go from one to the other, you had to go over a very narrow wooden bridge. Below, you could see the Aryan people strolling around. Life on the other side was different. **It was normal**.

Transition point for Jews only, over Chlodna Street. Polish citizens walked and rode under the bridge. The bridge was very narrow, and people sometimes waited for hours to cross it.

The Germans ordered 6,000 people to report to the rail station every day in order to be shipped to labor camps. They said these people were being relocated to the east. No one knew where the trains were going. The Jewish police would round up people to be shipped out. If you walked near the station, the Jewish police would grab you and put you on a train.

On the Aryan Side and The Warsaw Ghetto Rising

We hated living in the ghetto—this wasn't living. One day, as my mother and I escaped the ghetto to find food again, she said to me: "We're not going back." We took absolutely nothing with us. She had jewelry, but she didn't take it with her since we left on the spur of the moment. All we had were the clothes on our backs. I don't remember exactly when we left, I only know that it was wintertime and freezing.

We left without anywhere to go. In the past, when we had escaped to smuggle food, the custodian from our old apartment building would tell us that we could sleep at his place. You were not supposed to stay on the Aryan side, and you would be shot if you were caught. Once, when we had stayed at the custodian's place, a person came to his apartment and told him that someone had seen us and was considering reporting it to the Germans. So now the custodian was afraid and told us we could not sleep there anymore.

Since we had nowhere to go when we left the ghetto, we just started walking the streets. For a few days we slept under the steps of buildings, and in basements. One day while we were walking, we saw the woman from our old apartment building who hated us for being Jewish and to whom we had given the loaf of bread. She asked my mother what we were doing on the Aryan side. Very often, Poles would take people they knew to be Jews to the police station and turn them in. The Jews would be shot, and the Poles would receive payment for turning in the Jews. Warsaw was a big city, and since my mother had had a large clientele before the war there was always a chance we would be recognized by someone who knew her. You never knew who your friends or enemies were on the Aryan side. They were more friendly with money than with Jews.

We had no idea what our former neighbor might do when she saw us, since she had always hated Jews in general and us in particular. Mother told her we were looking for a place to stay and she said, "Come with me." There was a small building in the cemetery where she had an office, because she took orders there for headstones. She took us there to stay, and we remained with her for a couple of weeks. Every morning, she would come from her home with food to share with us. We couldn't stay there for a long time because we couldn't use the stove for heat at night, and it was freezing cold. The smoke from the chimney would have given away the fact that somebody was living there, and it would be suspicious for anyone to be staying at the cemetery at night. We could only have a fire during daylight hours when she was with us.

A loaf of bread - amazing how that could change a person from someone who despised Jews to someone who would risk her life to help us hide from the Nazis.

After some time, my mother found another place for us to stay, and it happened to be very close to the ghetto walls. The new place was owned by a woman she knew. I believe her name was Mrs. (Pany) Kazia Golianowa. I think it was located at 89 Wronia Street, but I am not sure. Her apartment was on the sixth or seventh floor, and there was no bathroom. The toilet was in the courtyard, so we could only use it at night. She had one big room and a kitchen. There was a trunk in the kitchen which we used as a bed. The trunk was four feet long and about two and a half feet wide, with a hump in the middle. Mother would sleep towards the wall, and I always slept towards the edge. Kazia's nephew would come over drunk, and always wanted to start something with my mother. He was also very friendly with the Germans. I always slept on my right side all night without moving - there was no space to move - and I used my hand as a pillow (we didn't have pillows). To this day, I still sleep on my right side and can't sleep with a pillow.

Kazia also had a grown son who lived with her, and he was crazy. Whenever I was left alone with him, he made inappropriate remarks, and he wanted me to touch him. He brought his friend over and wanted me to touch his friend as well. I hated him. I knew what he wanted me to do was wrong, so I always made excuses by making myself busy cleaning or doing other things. They laughed all the time, saying that all Jewish women are whores. It made me so mad, but I kept my mouth shut. I had no other choice.

Kazia also took in a boarder for extra money. In addition to all the people, Kazia had a beautiful white angora cat. The cat was accustomed to using the sink as its bathroom, then cover it with pieces of paper that were there for him to use. The boarder hated cats, and the cat sensed the hatred. Instead of using the sink, the cat began to do his business under the man's bed. The crazy son got mad and beat the cat, and when this didn't solve the problem, he threw the cat out the apartment window. When people say that a cat has nine lives, believe it. It is the truth. The cat landed on his feet and didn't even sustain an injury. He continued to go to the bathroom under the boarder's bed, and I would quickly clean it up.

During this period, I started to lose my baby teeth. I was in terrible pain and had a very high fever. There was an odor coming from my mouth that was so foul that no one could stand near me. Nothing could be done. I couldn't go to a doctor. I don't know how long I suffered, but it must have been at least a few weeks. At times my fever was so high they believed I was going to die, but eventually the infection passed.

Very early in the morning each day, a group of Jewish men, to include my uncle Zeilik, were taken from the ghetto to a forced labor site to work all day. When they were on their way back to the ghetto in the evening, exhausted, I would run to Zeilik and give him some food that he could share with my grandmother. I remember that one day, still during wintertime, there was a small girl at the place where we were waiting for Zeilik, maybe two or three years old, sitting near the gate on the Aryan side. She was so tiny that perhaps no one noticed her crawling out to the Aryan side from the ghetto. Her hair was black and her eyes were big and black. She looked like a little doll. She was just sitting there and crying. I said to my mother, "Let's take her." Mother said, "What do you want me to do? How can we take her when we don't know how long we will be where we are now? How can we help anybody when we don't know what will happen to us?" I started to cry, wondering why this was happening. How was it that I couldn't even help this small, defenseless little girl?

I was left alone at one point when my mother had to return to the ghetto. She had injured her finger which had caused an infection that developed into gangrene. She had no access to medical care on the Aryan side, so she was forced to go back into the ghetto. She was able to receive treatment there, where they removed her fingernail. She was lucky to be able to be treated, since there was no medicine available in the ghetto. She was also very lucky to have escaped the ghetto again.

There was an orphanage in the ghetto run by Janusz Korczak, who had come from a rich, assimilated family (Jews who did not practice the Jewish faith). He was a physician and a writer who wrote many children's books under this pen name, though his real name was Henryk Goldszmit. He'd been a military doctor with the Polish armed forces during the Russo-Japanese War, World War I, and the Polish-Soviet War, and had attained the rank of Major.

Korczak ran a Jewish orphanage and a Christian orphanage as well. Everyone in Poland knew who he was because he was a famous writer and he changed the way orphanges were run in Poland. In the 1900s, an orphanage was like a prison, but Janusz Korczak managed to change this situation. He made life meaningful for the kids who lived in orphanages. They felt like people as opposed to prisoners. They published their own newspaper, and participated in many other enriching activities.

Mother knew Korczak personally. When she was a little girl, her family had lived across the street from the orphanage at 81 Krochrmalna Street. Korczak used to come to my grandfather's apartment to pick up one of my mother's brothers and take him to summer camp and bring him home. Her brother was a very gifted child, but he died young.

On August 6, 1942, Janusz Korczak was ordered to report to the railway station (*umschlagplatz*), along with all of the Jewish orphans he was caring for. There were over 200 children. The underground wanted to save him, but he said, "I'm going where the children are going." They were sent to Treblinka, where all of them went straight to the gas chambers and perished that same day. I heard a story that when they were marching to the railway station, some of the children started to cry, and Stefania Wilczynaska, who had worked with Korczak, told them, "Don't cry. We are going on an outing."

Some people escaped from the camps and returned to the ghetto to try to warn people about what was really going on and where the trains had actually taken them. The Jewish committee (*Judenrat*), though, was unwilling to believe what they were told. This is not possible, they would say. The Germans are the most educated people in Europe. It was the younger people who believed that all those people leaving the ghetto by rail, supposedly to go to work camps, were really being sent to extermination camps.

After a period of four months of no deportations, the Germans entered the ghetto. Within hours, 600 Jews were shot and another 5,000 rounded up.

Korczak monument

There was a small uprising in the ghetto. The date was January 18, 1943. This particular uprising did not last long, but after, when I would go to the gates of the ghetto, I don't remember seeing Jews leaving for work again. But I am positive that I never saw my Uncle Zeilik after that. The big uprising started on April 19, 1943.

The young people inside the ghetto decided that if they were going to die, they would rather die fighting than go like sheep. They received some guns from the Polish underground, and were able to obtain some uniforms from a factory inside the ghetto where German uniforms were made. There was a rumor that some of the young people who spoke German would disguise themselves in German uniforms that they'd obtained. They would point out a building to the Germans and tell them that there were Jews hiding there. The Germans would go to the building, and Jews would ambush them and take their guns. The Germans sent a tank and heavy armored cars into the ghetto, which caught fire from Molotov cocktails thrown from upper windows and the roofs of the buildings. After that, German soldiers went house to house, burning the homes and capturing and killing the Jews.

One of my cousins, Marysia, was in a house with four other women. When the Germans saw the women, they took them to the roof of the house and told them to jump. Four of the women jumped from the building to their deaths. My cousin asked if she could jump from the other side of the building, which the Germans said she could do. So she jumped from the other side, caught hold of a pipe, and slid down to the ground.

When the Germans came down from the roof and saw her standing there, they told her they were going to send her to a camp. She was sent to Auschwitz Concentration Camp, and she survived. After the war, Marysia married my cousin Jakub Cienki in Israel. They have two daughters, Batia and Dalia. Marysia never told her daughters about what happened to her in the ghetto.

At night we could see from where we were staying that the sky over the ghetto was red. The ghetto was burning.

Jews leap from the upper floor of a blazing building. Stroop ordered that any fighter trying to escape be shot.

Sometimes I did stupid things without thinking. During the uprising, I once snuck out of the apartment and stood by the wall of the ghetto. I could hear shooting inside. I was crying, because even though I was young, I wanted with all my heart to be on the other side of the wall, inside the ghetto. I wanted to fight with the others. I was so proud that they stood up against the injustices that were being committed against us. I didn't care about anything else, I just wanted to fight. I didn't think what this might do to my mother, if I was able to leave. I had a powerful desire to join the fight.

While I was standing by the wall, a group of Polish boys, about six to eight of them, came over and saw me standing by the wall, crying. They figured I must be Jewish. They said, "In this building, there is a way through the basement that you can get into the ghetto." Of course, by the time I realized it was a trick, it was too late. They grabbed me and pulled me to the filthy floor of the basement. They were holding my hands and feet, and they started to jump on me one at a time. There was a noise which scared them, so they ran away. I cleaned myself up. I didn't know what rape was then, and for many years I felt guilty. I was afraid to say anything to my mother. I worried that she would be mad at me, but mostly I was mad at myself for being so stupid and naive.

That day I made myself a promise. I promised myself that I was going to survive no matter what; that I was going to be strong and that no one was ever going to see me cry again. That I would not trust people anymore. I had developed the mentality of a twenty year old. I went back to the apartment.

The order from Berlin. Eradicate any sign or memory of the Jewish presence in the ghetto. This is what was left of Gensza Street

The uprising was in April, 1943. The heavy fighting lasted for one month, but the fighting lasted past May. The Germans gave another order that if a Jew was found hiding in any of the buildings on the Aryan side, everyone living in the building would be shot. Kazia told mother that she couldn't keep us any longer. We left and found another place to hide. The woman who had the restaurant where we sometimes worked was living in a building on Chlodna Street (I think). On the floor above her, in an attic apartment, lived a woman named Zosia. She knew my mother from before the war, when she gave the woman manicures and pedicures. Zosia took us in without knowing whether or not we were Jewish. She may have suspected it, but the subject never came up. She had three rooms: one for her, one for us, and in the third room she ws raising rabbits. There was a window in the roof. I had to stay there by myself all day long, while mother worked, cleaning houses or whatever else she could find.

My mother's I.D. photo during the war

"Identity of this person Mrs. Karpinska Jadwica. Resides at St._____ No 11. This was written on the back of her photo."

A friend of ours was able to have my mother's photograph signed by somebody from City Hall. It identified my mother as Jadwiga Karpinska, who lost her real papers in the bombing of 1939. My name at the time was Basia. This was the only form of official identification that we had, and it meant nothing to a German. If a German had caught us, he would probably have shot us.

While mother was either working or looking for work, I was all by myself. I made little pillows. I also tried to make a radio. It consisted of two pieces of wood, and a wire with something like a crystal in the middle. I don't recall if it actually worked. I wanted to play with something, but I didn't have any toys. I tried to sneak into the rabbit room and catch a baby rabbit, but there was a daddy rabbit, a big and mean guy, and every time I would sneak in and try to grab a baby, he would come up behind me and bite my feet. One day Zosia decided to make rabbit stew. Boy, that stew was terrific, and I was one happy kid for two reasons. The first reason the stew was especially good because we didn't have much meat to eat, and if you were able to obtain any meat at all, it was only horse meat, so rabbit was a real treat. The second reason is that I could now play with the babies without fear of being bitten.

One day I decided to explore the bottom floor of the building, and saw the dirty windows of a carpenter's shop. It had probably been owned by a Jew, because no one worked there anymore. Somehow I found my way in. I loved the smell of the wood that lingered in the air. Once, when I went there I found another little girl there and we played together. That was my little companion, but only for a very short time. When I told my mother about the little girl, she and Zosia decided that I should be sent away. I've always wondered if Zosia knew we were Jewish.

Zosia had relatives who lived on a farm somewhere, I don't know exactly where it was. She decided that I should go for a short while and stay with them. I don't remember too much about that place. There was a woman and a man living there, and they baked black bread in a huge outdoor oven. That bread, with butter, was the best thing I had ever eaten. It was terrific. To this day, given the choice between bread and cake, I'm going to reach for the bread over the cake. I only stayed a few weeks. I don't know why I wasn't there very long, or why I was there in the first place, but when I returned home I was crawling with lice. Mother put a newspaper on the floor, ran a special comb through my long hair, and the lice landed on the newspaper. Then she put kerosene in my hair to kill the eggs, which made my eyes and scalp burn. I didn't go back to stay with those people anymore.

Zosia's brother brought a man to stay at her home. One day, as I was standing next to him, I heard him counting in Yiddish. I said to my mother, "You know he is Jewish." She replied, "You don't know what you're talking about." I told her again, "He is Jewish. I heard him count in Yiddish." Mother spoke with him, and told him that both of them could not stay in the same place. He asked why, and she said, "Because we are the same as you." He went to stay with Zosia's brother. We met him again in Israel after the war. I was right about him.

I was up in the attic by myself all day long. I found a Bible with lots of pictures. To pass the time, I started to learn how to read by comparing the words with the pictures. My mother helped me when she came home. Another book I became familiar with was an Esperanto language book. In 1887 Dr. Ludwig Zamenhof invented this language in hope that one day everybody would pick a common language. I started to learn Esperanto. (Today Esperanto is used in Eastern Europe and China.)

Every night prayers were held in the courtyard, in Polish and in Latin. I learned how to pray in both languages. It was very important to learn how to pray, because the Germans had a trick where they would ask you to cross yourself and pray. If you knew how to pray, they assumed you were Catholic.

I was desperate to go outside, so one day I just went out. Someone recognized me and asked, "Aren't you Blima's daughter?" I said, "No, I'm not," and started to walk away. The individual followed me, so I thought, "I have to lose this person somehow." I snuck into a movie house. The movie was an older version of Titanic. I saw part of it and then slipped out through the side door. I wasn't sure, but I had a feeling that I was still being followed, so I went and stood near a group of people and tried to blend in with them. They were gathered around two craters that were left from the bombings, and they were looking at the remains of a woman they said had been murdered. Her body was in one ditch and her head was in another.

Still not sure if I was being followed, I boarded a tram and went to see Zosia's friends. They lived in Praga, across the river. I decided that I would stay with them for a little while. I wasn't sure if they knew whether I was Jewish or not. All of a sudden it was curfew. I told them I had to leave, but they said, "No, it's already curfew. You have to stay." I was so nervous that I got a nose bleed and I bled all over their pillows. I woke up at 4 am, apologized for the nose bleed, and when the curfew was over I left to catch a tram home. It was still dark, and I needed to walk through a cemetery and a German post to get to that tram. I caught the first tram (streetcar), and when I got to the apartment building the gate was already open and my mother was so happy to see me that she didn't punish me. In normal times under those circumstances, I would have gotten a beating. While I was gone, someone came down through the window in the roof and stole a lot of different things. I was told that I wasn't to leave the attic anymore. My punishment was never being able to leave the apartment. I was locked in.

Some days later, as I was sitting in the attic room, I realized that someone was trying to get inside. I ran to the other window that was in Zosia's room and shouted, "Thieves! Thieves!" No one on the street could hear me because the apartment was too high up, but the would-be intruder heard me and ran away. There were no more break-ins after that.

Because the bathrooms were located in the courtyard, I was only able to use them when it got dark and when I was sure no other tenants were there.

The Polish Uprising and Russian Liberation

Introduction

By July 1944, Poland had been occupied by the Nazis for almost five years. The Polish Home Army, which was loyal to the Polish government-in-exile in England, had long planned some form of insurrection against the occupiers. Germany was fighting a coalition of Allied Powers, led by the United States, United Kingdom, and Soviet Union.

The initial plan of the Home Army was to link up with the invading forces of the Western Allies as they liberated Europe from the Nazis. However, in 1943 it became apparent that the Soviets, rather than the Western Allies, would reach the prewar borders of Poland before the Allied invasion of Europe made much headway. The Soviets and the Poles had a common enemy–Nazi Germany–but other than that, they were working towards different post-war goals. The Home army desired a pro-Western, democratic Poland; but the Soviet leader, Joseph Stalin, intended to establish a communist, pro-Soviet regime. It became obvious that the advancing Soviet Red Army might not come to Poland as an ally but rather as an occupier.

The situation came to a head on July 1, 1944, as the Soviet offensive crossed the old Polish border. At this point the Poles-in-exile had to make a decision: either initiate the uprising in the current difficult political situation and risk problems with Soviet support, or fail to rebel and face Soviet propaganda describing the Home Army as impotent or worse than the Nazi collaborators. In any case, the Soviet advance was so fast that Polish authorities saw no other choice but to continue the struggle against German forces and aid the Soviets.

Warsaw was chosen for the uprising partially because of its status as a pre-war capital. The Allies foresaw that the Germans would wish to hold onto Warsaw for as long as possible as a tool of morale, communications, supply and troop movement. Although there were air drops by American, British and Polish forces prior to and during the uprising, most supplies fell uselessly into German hands.

This left the Polish Home Army forces seriously under-supplied. The date for the Warsaw Uprising was set for August 1, 1944. The uprising was intended to last only a few days until Soviet forces arrived; however, this never happened, and Polish forces had to fight with little outside assistance. The uprising ended in capitulation to the Germans with the destruction of 85% of Warsaw and the deaths of over 250,000 civilians.

The Polish Uprising

In the summer of 1944, when the French were still waiting for the Americans to liberate Paris, in Warsaw the Polish resistance decided to rise up against the Germans. When the uprising began, we were all told to go down to the basements. The area of the basement that we stayed in was just a small cubicle near the steps that led to the basement. We had a little food and water, but it was slowly disappearing. I would go out and walk among the people, and when I did I would overhear things that they were saying. One story I heard was that a Jewish person went to some of the Polish resistance fighters and told them he was Jewish and wanted to help them fight the Germans. Instead, they shot him. I went back and told this story to my mother, as I did whenever I heard stories while I was out walking. I also heard horror stories of Germans shooting civilians and where the fighting was taking place. I heard people talking about how the uprising was going. All of this I told my mother, and it didn't seem like it was going so well.

One day, Zosia said she thought it would be better if she locked us in her basement cubicle from the outside. We were locked inside for a few days. When the Germans came, they threw a hand grenade down the steps into the basement where the people were staying safe, and shouted for everyone to get out, "*Raus, Raus!*" Mother said we had to stay because we didn't have papers. A few minutes later, someone returned and yelled in Polish that everyone had to get out of the basement because the Germans were going to set the building on fire. I told my mother that I'd rather get shot than be burned alive, and started kicking at the door over and over until it opened. The first thing I saw lying at the bottom of the steps was a small dog that had been hit by the hand grenade. It was still breathing.

We were lucky, because after the Germans returned they began pulling people from homes and shooting them, but by the time they got to our building they'd stopped killing civilians. We finally left our basement and started walking. We saw bodies lying everywhere in the streets. There was, of course, a German patrol checking identification papers. My mother told me to do something, so I started jumping up and down, yelling that I needed to go to the bathroom. There was an empty building on the side of the street, and one German said, "Go over there, do what you need to do, and then come back here." Instead of returning to him, we went around the patrol and started to walk with people who had already passed through the checkpoint.

The Germans put us in a large church on the outskirts of Warsaw. I don't remember Zosia being there, but mother told me she was, and that she was wounded. It was summer, and very hot. There was no food or water, but we were already accustomed to being without.

There was only one German watching over everybody in church. He was furious because he was scheduled to go on furlough to see his family in Berlin. He was screaming that Berlin was being bombed, and that his family was there. Hearing that Berlin was being bombed was very good news to us. He would hit whoever came near him with the butt of his gun, and he kept yelling and yelling. Then he got an order from his superior officer that we were being moved, and that people could start walking immediately if they wanted to, or they could wait until the next day. Of course, we were never told where we were going.

Mother told me to go ask the German if we should go as well, or if we should wait until the following day. I said to her, "He is going to kill me if I ask him." But for some reason, most of the time I was lucky. When I went to him to ask, he just patted me on the head and said, "Go today my child, because today it will be a slow march. Tomorrow it will be much worse." Mother went to Zosia and asked her if we should stay with her since she was wounded, but she told mother to go on without her.

By the time we got ready to leave, the doors to the church had been closed. They weren't going to let anyone else out, but the German told us he would let us out anyway, which he did. Outside the church, people were already lined up and ready to march, and we joined them. We started walking: women, elderly people, and children. We didn't see any teenagers or men in the group. We only had one soldier guarding us, riding around the column of people on a very large horse, making sure no one escaped. He wasn't a German; he was from Ukraine. Those were the worst kind, even worse than the Germans.

We walked on and on. I don't remember how long we walked, probably six or seven miles. We finally came to a little town where there was a rubber factory, part of which was being used as a hospital. All of the workers were Polish, but Germans were in charge of the place. They were standing on the side of the road, watching us. One of the factory workers, a woman, was staring at me, and said to my mother, "I will take this little girl to live with me." Mother replied, "What am I, a dog?" She told mother she would take her too, as long as no one interfered. We later learned that I reminded the woman of her niece, who had died in a fire a few years earlier.

She took us to a small office in the factory and disappeared. While we waited, someone gave us water to drink, and a German officer came in and asked us if we had a place to stay. Just then, the woman returned. The German officer decided that he didn't want us leaving the factory through the front, so he took us to the back of the factory-hospital and opened a small gate for us to go out.

The woman was living with her sister in one room of a small house with a garden. Her sister had the key but wasn't there, so we had to wait in the garden. While we waited, that Ukrainian rode his big horse toward us, shouting, "Any bandits from Warsaw here?" Mother was holding a basket with our belongings, which she quickly tossed into the bushes. We all yelled, "No, there are no bandits here."

The woman and her sister, Bronislawa and Gena, didn't know we were Jewish. I went to church every Sunday and prayed to prove to them that I was a "good Christian girl." The priests blessed me with holy water, and I took communion as well, wondering what the wafer tasted like and whether or not it could be used for food. To this day I remember how to say the sign of the cross in Polish and Latin.

Somebody needed to do something - to make money, to buy food, and so I took a box and poked a hole on each side of it, then put a string through the holes and slipped it over my head. I bought cigarettes and emptied them into my box, then sold the cigarettes at the factory/hospital. I was doing very well, and the other kids from the town were jealous of me. They would say, "She's so lucky. She must be Jewish." From that day on, I tried to be invisible.

One day I arrived late and saw all the other kids who sold cigarettes singing and dancing. I asked them what had happened to make them so happy, and they said, "Oh, they found a Jewish engineer and they shot him." He had good papers, but they told him to lower his pants and they saw that he was circumcised (because of their religion, Jewish men had to be circumcised). They knew he was a Jew, so they shot him. I saw a handkerchief nearby, and I picked it up. I kept that handkerchief for a long time just so I could remember what happened that day. I went to a corner where no one could see me, and I cried. I could not understand how kids could be so happy to see someone being killed, and I cried for that poor man.

Bronislawa's sister, Gena, befriended a German soldier. He used to come over sometimes and bring food with him. He talked about his family in Germany, and he saw that we didn't have a blanket, so he brought us one.

One day I found a little dog, a Pekinese. I took him in and kept him for a couple of weeks, sharing what little food I had with him; he got half of whatever I had. Then some people came to us and claimed that he was their dog. I didn't want to give him up and he didn't want to go to them, but mother said I had to give the dog to them or they might go to the police and we would be questioned. I remember the dog looking back at me as they took him away. He didn't want to go. My little bit of happiness was being taken from me.

The next door neighbor had an apple, a plum, and a cherry tree. No one was selling any fruit. Imagine how tempting those apples, plums and cherries were to me. At dusk, just before darkness came, I would climb a tree, and with the tree leaves covering me I would grab at the fruit. It didn't matter if an apple was green and unripe. I ate the whole thing anyway. I would eat plums and cherries, putting the pits in my pockets, and go find a hiding place. I would crack open the pits with a stone, or break them with my teeth, and I ate them too. Nothing was wasted. When the fruit ripened, and the neighbor went to pick the apples, plums and cherries, there was no fruit inside the trees, just on the outside. He never figured what happened to the fruit inside the tree, but he never caught me either. I had fun with that. To this day, I still crack cherry pits with my teeth and eat them.

I was a tomboy. If someone picked on me, I gave it right back to them. Mother would tell me that I couldn't do those things, but I didn't care. I was fed up with people picking on me. If someone gave me a hard time, I gave them a hard time right back. I used to defend smaller children and I played with them. One day I was giving a girl a piggyback ride, and I fell on the sidewalk and split my chin open. I went home and bandaged my chin by myself. I still have a small scar on my chin from this accident.

The German 3rd SS Panzer Tank Division came to town and remained there for awhile. They started to look for women to work in the kitchen, to peel potatoes and other things. My mother went and worked for them. One day an officer came and said that he needed someone to clean his room so mother did it. A short time later, a high ranking officer came and asked who was cleaning the other officer's room. Everyone said it was Jadwiga. He liked her work so much that he told her she was going to clean his rooms as well. (What a big honor!)

The Germans didn't pay in currency - payment was that the working women's children would get any soup they had left over. The kids would come with cooking pots and lids to take the soup home. I always tried to be first in line, because the first person would sometimes get a little meat and potatoes. All the good stuff was at the bottom of the pot, which the cook would dish out with a ladle. So the first person always got the best soup.

There was always a guard watching over the soup line. One day, as I was standing in line, I was laughing, and a new guard didn't like it. He told me to go to the end of the line. I started to curse him in German, and he really didn't like that, so he picked me up and was about to throw me down the nearby well. Luckily for me, another German came and told him to leave me alone.

The Germans disappeared from town quite suddenly. No one knew what was happening at the time, but the reason was that the front was getting close. It was hard to get any food, even bread. Occasionally we would find some bread, but for some reason it smelled and tasted like kerosene. It was awful, but your choice was to eat it or starve.

Russian Liberation

A rumor circulated that Russian tanks were in Pruszkow, the town next to ours. (During the 1944 Warsaw Uprising, the Nazis had created a transit camp in Pruszkow to hold people evacuating from Warsaw. From August to October 1944, approximately 650,000 people passed through the camp, where the Nazis segregated them. 55,000 were sent to various concentration camps, including 13,000 sent to Auschwitz. It was our good luck that Bronislawa had pulled us out of of the group we were marching with.)

When I heard that Russian tanks were there, I ran to Pruszkow to see. It was true: there were Russian tanks with big red stars painted on their sides. People were already sitting on top of them. I jumped on the second or third tank as they were rolling towards the town I lived in. When they got to our town, people were standing on the street waiting. Could it be true? Had the Germans really gone? Mother was among the people in the streets. She was thinking I was going to go all the way to Warsaw on the tank, but of course they wouldn't take anyone past Piastow, where we were living.

The tanks rolled on toward Warsaw. Every day, more and more Russian troops passed through our town. One Russian soldier passing through wore a big poncho that went down to the ground, and my mother started to talk with him because he looked Jewish to her. "Are you Jewish?" she asked him. He told her that he was, in fact, and she said, "I am Jewish too. What should I do?" He told her that for the time being she should just sit quietly, not say anything to anyone, but that the Germans were finished for sure. He or another soldier told her how to recognize if a person was Jewish: in a conversation, use the word "*Amhu.*" A Jew will know what it means. *Amhu* is a Hebrew word that means "His people."

On the day I heard the Germans were finished, I stopped going to church. My mother didn't have to tell me to do this, I did it on my own. I knew in my heart who I was. I was a Jew! I also changed my name from Basia to Wanda. I told everyone that this was going to be my new name, that this was going to be a new beginning in my life.

More and more Soviet troops arrived in Piastow, because this was their temporary headquarters.

Mother took over my business of selling cigarettes to the Russians, and added Russian newspapers. I wanted to join the girl scouts, but to join you had to have a uniform. There was a Russian general who wanted to adopt me and take me to Russia, and he gave me material to make a uniform. So I joined the girl scouts. I don't know how long I was in the girl scouts, or what we did, but I know I became a girl scout. Maybe I wanted that so much because my uncle Aron had been a boy scout leader, and I felt it was something to do in his memory.

Some of the Jewish Russian officers found out we were living in a room with other people. They told my mother that if she could find something better, they would arrange for us to move. We found a place, a house with three rooms, and they arranged for us to move.

There was an old woman living in one of the other rooms. Every time she walked by our room, she passed excessive amounts of gas that went on forever. The noise was constant and awful. I wanted to say something to her about it, but she was hard of hearing. Another woman and her daughter lived in the third room. The mother was from America, but was stuck in Poland during the war. We all shared the kitchen. There was an outhouse that was quite a distance from the house.

When the Russians went to Warsaw, they cleared the city of all the mines the Germans had placed. Different Jewish organizations opened offices for people to register and search for relatives who had possibly survived and were returning from labor or concentration camps. People were pouring into the city. We went there as well to have our names registered on the list of Holocaust survivors.

After liberation. My mother and I in Girl Scout uniform

The city of Warsaw was in ruins. I was looking at the spot where the ghetto had once stood and there was nothing there anymore. Mother and I went to the Jewish cemetery to look for grandfather's grave, but we couldn't find it because all the monuments and gravestones had been broken. I think the cemetery was on Gensia Street, but I am not sure.

Mother got a job working in a cafeteria that belonged to one of the Jewish political parties. She was the manager of the kitchen and dining area. They served lunch and dinner to people returning from the camps and from Russia. Sometimes at the cafeteria, someone would put a whole chicken in front of me and people would make bets as to whether I could finish it. The people who bet in my favor won every time.

In addition to her management job, mother and I also received help from Mr. Avraham and Mrs. Stela Zumoff, a couple from Brooklyn, New York. He worked for *The Forward*, a Jewish newspaper. Middle-class Jews were "adopting" survivors, and the Zumoffs adopted us. They would send us packages of food, and when mother asked them to send her a machine she could use to repair nylon stockings, they sent it. She repaired stockings for other people as well.

One day, as I was walking in our town, I saw a person walking and he began to ask me all sorts of questions. I looked at him and said. "You are uncle Henry!" I still knew who he was after so many years. He'd

With polish soldiers

been searching for family after he returned from Russia, and had found our names in the registry. He told us that he'd been sent from Moscow to Siberia for some reason. The Russians they didn't need much of a reason to send a person to Siberia. But Henry survived. Then he told us about the fate of my father. Both Henry and my father had left Poland in 1939. Henry had learned that my father was returning to Poland, but the Germans caught him near the city of Bialistock and shot him. That is how I found out what happened to my father, and at this point I really didn't care. My father never said goodbye to me when he left, and my mother knew that he'd been shot but never told me. Uncle Henry had already contacted grandmother Rose in the United States and was waiting for tickets and a place on a ship to get to her.

I got very sick after I went sledding without a jacket. When my mother took me to a doctor, he said I needed a different kind of environment, that I needed a drier climate. So they sent me to a sanatorium in Westergestor, in the mountains. This was a region that at one time had belonged to Poland, then Germany took it over, then Poland took it back. When the Germans had occupied it, there was a labor camp not far from the sanatorium. We went there many times. The sanatorium was only for Jewish children of all ages. Some of the children didn't have parents. The doctors and nurses took excellent care of us. In addition to recovering from our physical illnesses, we were educated and kept busy all the time. All the teachers were Jewish and one of them taught us about Jewish history. He did such a terrific job presenting this that it felt like you were actually living it. We spent all day learning because we had to make up for lost time.

We were supposed to drink milk to improve our health, but for some reason I hated milk. Four of the boys tried to force me to drink it, holding my arms and trying to hold my mouth open, but they didn't succeed. Of course, this was just done in fun. I was laughing that one little girl could beat four boys. I think my dislike for milk began when I was very little and my mother made me drink goat's milk. From that day on, I hated milk. The people at the sanatorium just wanted to help me, to make me stronger, but they never succeeded in making me drink milk. Remember, I was very stubborn. Every time I tried to drink milk I felt sick to my stomach.

The Sanatorium

There were two or three girls assigned to a room. There was one girl who was much older than the rest of us who would tell us stories when the lights went out. It was very nice. After all the bad times that we had gone through, it was a comfortable way to live. No one spoke about the past, and nobody wanted to remember it either. We wanted to live normal lives.

I started collecting stamps as a hobby. Every time I got a stamp from a different country, I would go to a map to see where the country was. That is how I practiced and learned geography.

After more than a year, I was told that I was healed and it was time to leave. I wanted to go. More than a year was long enough. One of the grown-ups was going to leave the sanatorium, and I asked if I could go with him. I didn't own a suitcase, so I filled two boxes with my belongings. There was a German man working as a driver who took us to the railroad station. The box containing my entire stamp collection broke and I asked the driver if he could send it to me. He promised he would, but he never did, and this is how I lost my entire stamp collection. I was so angry about losing this collection. One more black mark for the Germans.

After returning from the sanatorium, mother and I went to visit Uncle Henry's friends who lived in the city of Lodz, where there was a kibbutz/orphanage. It wasn't like a kibbutz (a collective living community) in Israel. This was a city kibbutz. The director was Pawel, a tall, skinny man who wore glasses. He looked older, and he had a limp. I found out later that he had fought as a partisan against the Germans, and was wounded. He lost his entire family.

Pawel told my mother that they were taking care of children, and encouraged her to leave me there. He was very friendly and he looked to me like a nice person, so I decided that if I liked it, I would stay. It was an apartment with a few rooms. There was a housekeeper - I think her name was Mania - and she was very nice. I was in the younger group. After school hours, they taught us about Palestine. A man by the name of Jankale, who was a gymnast, taught us sports. He was with the group of grownups that lived separately from us. I was very strong and athletic, and Jankale wanted me to be a gymnast. I liked sports, but not as a profession, and my bones were no longer flexible enough. He taught me all sorts of things, but I was more interested in books.

I was involved in all sorts of activities at the kibbutz. We had a choir that traveled to many locations, and I was a soloist. Then the group decided to go to the Polish port of Gdansk. From there we traveled to an island called Westerplatte. This island has the unhappy distinction of being the site of the official start of World War II. While we were on the ship headed there, everyone from my group was seasick. No one could hold down any food. I was taking care of a sack of apples, and while everyone else was getting sick I was lying on a bench with the sack under my head, having a great time and eating the apples one after another.

At some point, the older group from the kibbutz was preparing to leave for Palestine, and the younger group was going to follow shortly thereafter. I wanted to go, but my mother said no. She came to pick me up and took me to Warsaw. Grandmother Rose wanted me to go with the group, because they went through France on the way to Palestine. Grandmother Rose wrote in a letter that if I went to France, she would come for me and take me back with her to the United States. I said, "No way. If I'm going anywhere, I'm going to Palestine."

On April 19, 1948, while I was in Warsaw, a monument was dedicated to the courageous Warsaw ghetto fighters. The Warsaw ghetto was one of 100 recorded Jewish revolts against the Nazis. During the dedication ceremony, there was a large procession that included flowers and wreaths. I was one of the people in that procession, and I placed a wreath at the base of the monument. The artist who created the monument was Nathan Rapoport, a native of Warsaw.

Procession to memorialize the courageous Warsaw Ghetto fighters.

The flowers I put on the monument

Ghetto fighters on the monument to the Ghetto Heroes

After the kibbutz, my mother found an orphanage/children's home which was in Otwock, southeast of Warsaw. The orphanage had been bombed at the beginning of the war. Only children who had either one parent, or no parents, were able to live there, so that's where I was sent. I remember one day I went to a pond and I was pretending I knew how to swim, which of course I didn't. There was a family there and the father had an inner tube. I asked if I could borrow it. I was acting very confident about my non-existent swimming abilities. I began to imitate the swimmers, but the damn inner tube slipped out of my grasp and floated to the surface. As I was going down, I looked up and could see the sun shining. I thought, "I'm either going to sink or swim." So I began kicking my feet and I rose to the surface. As I got to the surface, I grabbed the inner tube and gave it back to the father. Then I started swimming. That is how I learned to swim. Years later I taught my cousin, Dovik, to swim, in Israel. He went to serve in the navy.

In the children's home we learned many things. There was a piano in my room and my mother wanted me to take piano lessons, but I didn't want to. Now I wish I had listened to her. I was taking ballet lessons, but one day a fight broke out over a slipper. I joined in to help, but unfortunately tripped on the slipper and broke my leg in four places. That was the end of my ballet career.

The orphanage had a watch dog, a large German Shepherd with his own dog house in the backyard. Everyone was afraid of him. I used to go into his dog house with a book and he would lie down in front of me and watch over me while I read. No one could see me or find me. I did have friends, good friends, but I didn't like to be disturbed. I preferred my own company, and the company of the dog and books. I belonged to three libraries. You could only take two books from each library at a time. If I couldn't be out in the dog house, then I would lie under my bed with a flashlight and read. Mother would send me money to buy fruit, but the money went to buy books.

The teacher at the school was the biggest anti-Semite there ever was. And this was after the war. All the other kids at the school would say a prayer every day. Jews didn't pray, but we were made to stand up with everyone else. I hated that teacher, and her daughter. Her daughter was "the best student in the class." This was what her mother, our teacher, would tell us. We had to learn Russian at school. Now we were dealing with the communists.

One of the school's requirements for girls was that we had to learn how to knit. But I had a difficult time learning, so I asked if I could go with the boys, whose requirements included woodworking. Later on in life, this came in handy; I knew how to make my own cabinets.

One of my friends and I did puzzles and sent them to newspapers, but we never won. I am still friends with some of the children that I met at this orphanage. Some live in Israel.

While I was at the orphanage, mother completed the paperwork to leave Poland and immigrate to Israel. The United Nations resolution of November 1947 divided the already cut up Palestine into two sectors: one Jewish and the other for a new state of Palestinian Arabs. The day after the U.N. resolution was adopted, Arab violence against Jews, which had been almost non-existent for some time, erupted throughout Palestine almost as if by signal. Organized bands of Arabs killed Jewish men, women, and children. Arab snipers took aim at Jewish buses on highways. The mastermind behind the undeclared war against the Jews by Arabs was Hajj Amin al-Husaayni, the Mufti of Jerusalem.

In May, 1948, a new state was established. The State of Israel. This was where we wanted to go, but we had to wait from 1948 until the beginning of 1950. That is when we finally got permission to leave Poland. My mother and I had to sign papers stating that we were no longer Polish citizens. We had papers that were similar to a passport. It didn't say that our nationality was Polish, it said that we were Jewish. I still have mother's and my own documents.

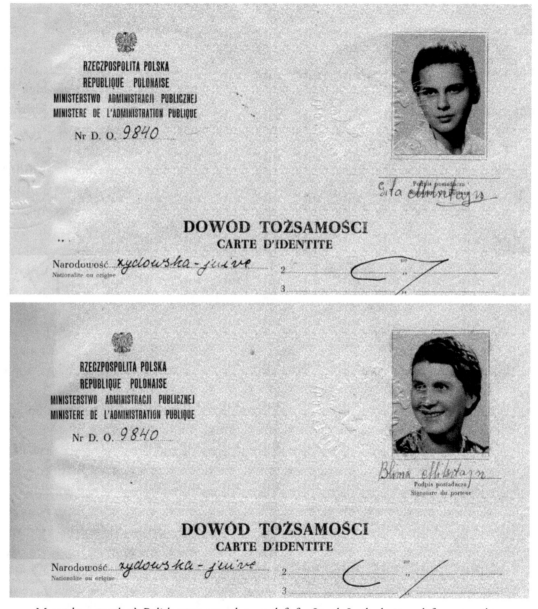

My and my mother's Polish passports when we left for Israel. In the bottom left corner, they announce our nationalities as being Jewish instead of Polish.

If I felt any sorrow for leaving Poland, it was only for a brief moment. I only had to remind myself how my teacher looked at me with such hatred in her eyes, and I did not feel sorry for leaving the country called Poland. I never understood how it was the Poles could hate a Jew, and yet they prayed to a Jew and believed in him.

When you left Poland, you were not allowed to take any cash or gold with you. So we had to smuggle some out. Mother had a goose feather quilt that we stuffed with American dollars that Grandmother Rose had sent us. We rolled the dollars up with tape and threw them inside the quilt. I had a gold bracelet that I hid inside an iron. I took the iron apart and taped the bracelet inside so it didn't rattle. We took linens, and we loaded all of our belongings into wooden crates. And then we boarded a train. We were finally leaving. Ours was the second group to leave Poland.

The day I left Poland was one of the happiest days of my life. I felt like nothing had changed there and that the war had not taught them a thing. As we passed through the countryside, I felt such an incredible sense of happiness. Poland was my country, but I did not feel anything for it. I was hated here; my family had been murdered here. Of course, not all the Poles were bad, but too many of them helped the Germans. Most of the concentration camps were built in Poland. The Polish underground did not do enough to help the ghetto fighters. When the Jews began returning from the concentration camps and coming out of hiding, they went to their homes to try to reclaim their property and valuables. Instead of returning the looted items to their rightful owners, as other nations did, the Poles killed many of the survivors. In other countries, when survivors returned they found their belongings intact. This is why, even after the war, I didn't care for the Poles. They hadn't changed. I don't know if they are still like that today. Once I left Poland, I never went back.

I hadn't known ahead of time, but two other kids from the children's home were also on the train. We already had a pact. The three of us, Hana, Jurek, and me, went everywhere together. From Poland we went through Czechoslovakia and Austria to the port of Genoa, in Italy. From there we took an Israeli ship, with Israeli sailors on board, with the Israeli flag flying. I made friends with one of the sailors right away, and we are still friends to this day. He tried to teach me Hebrew, which wasn't an easy language to learn in such a short time, but I managed to learn a few words.

It was not very comfortable on the ship. There was a large berth with bunches of beds and people sleeping next to you and above you. It was May and it was hot. I spent most of my time on the deck.

For the first time in my life, when I boarded the ship I felt like I was a free person. Not knowing what was in store for me, I felt free. I felt a sense of belonging. This was where I wanted to be. Watching the Israeli sailors, how they acted, was like watching a different world. They were not scared people. We were not surrounded by scared people any more. It was such a relief, and such an unbelievable feeling. The food on the ship was lousy, but I didn't care. The feeling of freedom was more important to me than anything in the world.

I don't remember how many days it took us to arrive at Haifa port, but I could have sailed forever.

Israel

The last night on the ship, as we neared the shores of Israel, I couldn't sleep. In the early morning, the city of Haifa appeared in front of us. Haifa is built on top of Mount Carmel, so it was a breathtaking view! I looked and looked and could not get enough of this vision. We arrived at the port, descended from the ship, and were taken by vehicle to a transit place called Tira, which was not far from Haifa. From Tira they would place people at towns throughout the country.

My problem with Tira was that it was surrounded by barbed wire. There was a gate, and a guard to make sure no one left without permission. I said, "Heck, I'm not going to take this." So one day Jurek and I decided to take a walk to Haifa. Hana had chickened out. We snuck through the barbed wire and walked, and walked. The month of May is very hot in Israel.

We eventually came to a "mahbara," a place where people who'd gone through Tira were assigned to stay until housing was found for them. We stopped to ask a young girl how far it was to Haifa, but she spoke Hebrew and we only knew German, Russian, Polish and Yiddish. She called her mother to come talk to us and we asked the mother how much farther it was to Haifa. The mother spoke Polish, and asked if we were planning to walk the whole way there, saying it was still quite a distance away. After discussing the matter, we decided to go back to Tira.

They delivered the wooden crate with our belongings to us, but it was damaged. Water had gotten into the crate and we lost many of our things.

My name changed again, this time to a Hebrew name, Tova, which means good. Because I don't think I'm good, I did not like that name. However, to this day friends still call me Varda or Wanda. From Tira, we were sent to a mahbara located in Pardes Hanna, where we slept in a big tent with many other people. This might be considered fun for boy scouts or girl scouts, but we did not enjoy it. There was no choice, though.

Summer in Israel is similar to summer in Arizona, but in addition to the heat there is humidity. I slept in front of the tent most of the time. We knew that we had family in Israel because some of our relatives had left for Palestine after World War I. They had come to Warsaw and visited grandfather on their way to Palestine. So my mother started to search for the family, which took a while. We did, however, finally find them.

Grandfather's sister had left for Palestine with another sister's daughter, Rahel, when her mother passed away. My great aunt, Yaffa, had a son named Haim and a daughter named Rahi, who eventually married Arie, a Holocaust survivor from Holland who had survived Auschwitz. (Arie worked as a radio operator on Israeli merchant ships, and was later recruited by the Mossad. Several years later, when the Popular Front for the Liberation of Palestine hijacked a French airliner with Israelis onboard and landed it at Entebbe, Uganda, Arie was working in Entebbe as a radio operator, and was able to provide radio support in some way to the Israelis.) Rahel had one son, Dovik. All children who are born in Israel are called Sabras. A sabra is the fruit from a cactus we know as the prickly pear. It is sweet on the inside, but rough on the outside. I was the one who taught Dovik how to swim, and he later joined the Israeli Navy and was involved in underwater demolition.

Our family lived in Haifa. At a reunion, I saw the woman who I had spoken to at the mahbara when Jurek and I were walking to Haifa. Malka Szturman was her name. If I had happened to ask her name when we spoke, I would have recognized that her name was the same as my mother's maiden name. We were related – she was married to my grandfather's brother's son, who was named Mordechai. They survived the Holocaust by going to Russia. Malka and Mordechai have two children, daughter Rina and son Shlomo. (Shlomo eventually became a paratrooper. During the Six Day War, his unit was involved in retaking Jerusalem from the Jordanians, and he was one of the first to get to the Western Wall.)

I was sent to Alyiat Hanoar, a place for teenagers. I worked as an assistant to the doctor there, sort of like a nurse. I had been working there for a while when a group of kids from Switzerland came through to be examined prior to going to a kibbutz. One kid was left behind, because he was sick. When he got healthy, I took him to the kibbutz.

For some reason I liked the kibbutz and said that I wanted to go there too, Arie, (not my cousin) who was in charge of Aliat Hanoar begged me not to go to that kibbutz. He said he would send me to a better one. But I was stubborn and I insisted on going. I ended up hating it there. I was supposed to work a half day and study a half day, but they made me work more than study. They gave me a bible so I could memorize it in Hebrew, a language that was not easy to learn. Asking me to memorize it was asking a lot. I was working and learning. I hated it. Mother, in the meantime, lived for some time in Haifa with Rahel. She eventually left and went to live in Jaffo, near Tel Aviv. This was where she met her second husband. They were married in 1951 and she moved into his apartment. I hated the jerk, and believed she could have found someone much better.

On Friday evenings in Jaffo, people would walk through the streets. When I would go there to visit my mother, I would meet with my friends, the older group I'd been with back at the kibbutz/children's home in Lodz, Poland. Some of them could not find jobs and life was not easy. Some were thinking of leaving Israel for good. I had this sense of security knowing that everyone was Jewish and that people could safely walk in the streets at two in the morning. I felt free. There were roads that we had to avoid, however, because the Arabs would shoot at us. Despite that fact, there was a wonderful sense of community. Everyone was family. Everyone was in the same boat. No one had any money, it was hard to find work because everyone was immigrating at once from Europe and from the rest of the world. There was food rationing, one egg per person per week, but I didn't care because freedom meant everything to me. And I was free.

I hated life in the kibbutz. I hated it so much that whenever I had a day off I went to the military recruiting office. I wanted to join the army, but the recruiters told me that I was too young. I was just 17 at the time. In Israel, you had to serve in the military when you reached the age of 18. I kept going back, and eventually they got so tired of me that they told me I could join the military if my mother signed a consent form. I took the papers to my mother and she said, "No, you are too young. Wait until you are 18." I told her that if she didn't sign the papers, I would forge her signature and join the military with or without her permission. So she signed the papers, and I went to basic training.

My only fear was that I might get assigned to a unit that was going to be working on a kibbutz. There were quite a few units doing that. When I went to the basic training camp, one of the officers there was a cousin of mine from my father's side, Rina. (Rina married Kalman Magan, who became a Major General and one of Israel's youngest officers to fight in the war of independence. He also fought in the Six Day War and the Yom Kippur War. In one battle, he was wounded but continued to command until all of his soldiers had departed. Kalman was awarded the Chief of Staff Citation, which was later converted to the Medal of Valor. In the Yom Kippur War, he commanded the northern section. In the Sinai battles, his division launched diversionary attacks in Egypt to draw attention away from bridges being built at the Suez Canal. Kalman passed away of a heart attack on March 10, 1974. At his funeral, my husband Gerry and I stood on one side of the grave, and on the other side was Menachem Begin, Golda Meir, and Moshe Dayan. It was sad to see such an accomplished man laid to rest at such a young age.)

But back to basic training. My cousin Rina took me under her wing. I was still required to do everything just like everyone else. I had to learn to take a gun apart, I had to clean the latrines. Men and women were trained separately. I was in training for three months during the wintertime, which is rainy season in Israel. So there was mud everywhere. Once I had completed basic training, I was sent to military police courses. The camp was located near Haifa, in Tira, and this training was also three months long. An officer and I were in charge of the group. I had to get up every morning at 4:00, comb my long hair, and take the group for a run.

When I finished that training, I was assigned to a military police K-9 unit. Most of the time I worked with a veterinarian by the name of Doctor Kuperman, assisting with surgery on the dogs. The first time I assisted in surgery, it was for a dog with gallstones. When Doctor Kuperman opened him up, there was a lot of blood. The doctor looked at my face, which was white from seeing all the blood and the dogs' insides. He asked me if I was going to faint, but I said no, and I didn't. We removed the gallstones, sewed the dog back up, and all was well. After that first surgery, it became a no-brainer. I enjoyed taking care of the sick dogs and taking care of Kohba (Star), the black Belgian Shepherd with a white star on her chest who'd been assigned to me. I had always wanted to be a veterinarian, but we did not have the money for school.

Every year, around April or May, Israel celebrates Independence Day with a parade. Our unit participated in the 1952 parade, which happened to be in Tel Aviv. The dog that was walking behind me was a crazy German shepherd. He jumped on my back and bit me. I was bitten two more times by two different dogs. A photographer from a Swiss magazine was present at the 1952 parade, and took my picture. One of my friends saw the photograph on the cover of the magazine, and gave me a copy. I had not been aware that the picture had been taken until she gave it to me. We were in the parade again the following year, but it was in Haifa that time.

Most of my time in the service was spent working at the clinic, but I also trained some of the dogs. They served as watch dogs. On my days off, a friend who was an officer used to take me to Tel-Aviv on his motorcycle, and then back to the base. He never missed any potholes on the roads and my behind was sore from bouncing up and down by the time we got to Tel-Aviv and returned to the base.

I heard that the road to Sdom had been completed (1953), and I wanted to go there to see the Dead Sea. Sdom is the gateway to the Dead Sea, which has such a strong concentration of salt that you cannot swim in the water, you just float on top of it. I contacted a friend who had a motorcycle, and he agreed to take me. We found out that 67 kilometers of the road had actually been finished, but the last 10 kilometers were not. When we arrived to the point where there was no longer a paved road, my friend

1952 Israel Independence Day parade
Photo from the cover of Swiss magazine.
Original caption read: "*Militärhunde mit
ibren Betruern paradieren hier zur Feier
von Israels nationalem Unabhängigkeitstag.*

With my dog Kohba (Star). 1952

Independence Day parade, Tel-Aviv, Israel, 1952

Independence Day parade, Haifa,
Israel, 1953

said, "Let's turn back." I said, "No way. Let's go to the end." We continued on down the unfinished, unpaved portion of the road. The construction workers could not believe that two idiots on a motorcycle were trying to drive the unfinished road. We did successfully arrive at our destination, and we were the first motorcycle to get to the Dead Sea at that time. On the way back, I was so tired that I couldn't keep my eyes open. The road was empty for miles with nowhere to rest, so I asked my friend to stop and fell asleep in a ditch. After awhile, we continued on.

When Moshe Dayan was promoted to Chief of Staff, he decided that our unit should be disbanded. I was sent to serve in Nazareth, where there was a big English police station that had been taken over by the Isaeli Army northern command. We were responsible for patrolling the area in jeeps. We also had checkpoints, because anyone who was leaving one of the Arab villages at that time had to have a pass. We watched for people from some of the villages who were suspicious or could potentially cause harm to our population. Terrorism became an every day policy.

One evening, three of us were on patrol together. We stopped a truck full of watermelons at the top of a hill. Two of us, one of the guys and myself, went to check the driver's papers. The third guy suddenly had a taste for watermelon, but instead of asking for one, he went to the back of the truck and took one out. The idiot put the watermelon down on the ground and it started to roll underneath the truck and then down the hill, in front of the truck. The driver and the two of us watched in amazement as this watermelon continued to roll down the hill. The third guy never did get to eat watermelon, but he did get screamed at by us for doing stupid things.

I remember that once a member of the Knesset (Israeli Parliament), who happened to be an Arab communist, was coming to Nazareth with the intention of conducting a rally. We received an order that he was not allowed to hold the rally. When I had finished my duty at the checkpoint I had been assigned to, one of the officers asked if I wanted to go over to another checkpoint because they had spotted the Knesset member there. He was stopped and not allowed to enter. After this, I returned to my post and my duties. A bus full of passengers came up to my checkpoint. Three other soldiers from the reserves were with me. They checked the bus and said that everything was okay, but for some reason, I decided to check it again to make sure. As I went through the bus, I saw the Knesset member sitting in one of the seats. I asked him nicely to get off the bus, and he refused. You were not allowed to touch a Knesset member. At first I didn't know what to do, but then I asked everyone else to get off the bus. Once they had, I told the driver to turn around and return to where he had come from. So I didn't touch the Knesset member, but I managed to prevent him from going into town. It was my duty as the person in charge to stop him at the check point, and I had no love for communists because I'd come from communist Poland

Me during my service in the army

I had planned to meet with friends in Haifa one evening, but a general came to give a lecture so we had to stay put. I attended the lecture, and by the time it was over, the buses had already left the area. I went out to the gate to see if I could catch a ride with someone, and saw a friend sitting on his motorcycle. I said to him, "Let's go to Haifa." He told me that he had come with a friend so there was no room for me on the motorcycle, but that wasn't going to stop me because I needed to get to Haifa. So we went - three on a motorcycle. Of course I did not want to be lodged between two guys, so I was sitting at the back, almost on top of the wheel.

As we were descending down the hill to Haifa, a car passed us with some of the guys from the military police unit. They recognized me and yelled at me. I shouted for them to stop. I wanted to get into their car since my behind was sore from the ride. The driver of the car was moving pretty slowly and we were driving slowly as well. My friend driving the motorcycle yelled, "Don't stop! I ...." He never got to finish telling them that he didn't have brakes. When the motorcycle hit the car, I flipped into the air and landed on the road. I was laughing - it was just so funny. The driver of the car got out to check if his car had been damaged. Nothing had happened to the car or to the bike. I got into the back seat of the car, and we continued on our way.

After some time, one of the guys in the car said, "Hamefaked" (sir), which is the way you address an officer, "will you please stop here." I rose from my back seat, looked at the driver and thought, "Oh shit!" This was the general who had given us the lecture earlier that evening. I asked him to let me off at a certain point near my destination, and thanked him. The next day my commanding officer called me into his office and asked me if it was true that I had been riding with two additional people on a motorcycle. I said yes, and he told me not to do it again, that as a military police person I should know better. And then we both laughed about it.

The next place that I served at was a military police station in Haifa. We walked the streets in pairs there, checking to make sure soldiers who came to the city had gotten passes to leave their bases, and we made sure that they were dressed properly. I used to catch so many soldiers breaking the rules. Haifa is a port city and the Navy was stationed there. While I was busy writing out reports on them, they were busy asking me to go to the movies with them.

I was discharged from the army after serving my time. When I was in the service, my hair was very long and I would braid it and put it up on top of my head. Once I got discharged, I cut my hair short.

A friend of mine who was in the navy invited me to visit his ship. Many of the sailors asked me, "are you the MP (military police) who wrote me up?" I would say, "No, not me. That was my sister."

I needed to find a job after I was discharged from the army. I had experience working with military dogs, and because I loved animals in general I was able to find a job working as a zookeeper at the Tel-Aviv Zoo.

Tel-Aviv Zoo

I was staying at my mother's house in Jaffo. One night when I was sleeping, I felt someone touching me. I opened my eyes and there was my mother's husband, sitting on my bed, touching me. I jumped off the bed, grabbed my scout knife, and stabbed the SOB in three or four places. Luckily for the pig, the knife was not very sharp, but he bled a lot from the wounds. The next day I moved to my friend Hanna's house for a few days, until I found and rented an apartment of my own on Raines Street in Tel-Aviv. To call him a pig is an insult to the animal. From that day on I never spoke to him.

I took courses in economics at night, and singing lessons from a Jewish Egyptian professor of music. I also had to fulfill my duty in the army reserves every year. It usually lasted a month, but sometimes it was longer. The Suez Canal War broke out in 1956, and I was activated into the army reserves and assigned to Gaza.

The war started because the Fedayeen, a terror organization, had been crossing into Israel from Gaza and Jordan and raiding settlements. In the interest of assuring Israel's survival and the safety of its citizens, the government was obligated to act. On October 24, 1956, Egypt, Jordan and Syria established a joint military pact to destroy Israel. Israel's decision was swift. On October 29, Operation Kadesh began. Under the command of Moshe Dayan, the Israeli armed forces began to move into Sinai and obtained their objectives within one week, destroying Fedayeen bases and the blockade of the Gulf of Eilat at the Strait of Tiran.

France and Britain had attempted to take back the Suez Canal after Egyptian President Nasser nationalized it. Under pressure from the United Nations and threats from the United States and the Soviet Union, France and Britain withdrew. A cease fire took effect on November 5, and the Israelis eventually withdrew.

I went as far as El-Arish with the Israeli forces, but it wasn't safe there so they sent me back to Gaza. By the way, El-Arish is on the Mediterranean, and has beautiful white sand beaches. In Gaza, one of my responsibilities was to look after the prisoners of war during the day. At night, I performed guard duty at the main gate to the base. I used to be so stupid. I was never afraid of anything. People on duty with me would say, "I'm so tired," and I would tell them to go to sleep, which left me by myself. Luckily nothing ever happened. Those were just some of the duties that I had in the reserves. Other duties I will not mention.

The War of 1956, Gaza

To the United States, Israel and Back to U.S.

I had a cousin who lived in the United States, Jack Solomon, who was one of my grandmother's nephews. Jack had been born in the United States, and owned a bathing suit factory and was involved in other business ventures. He was very rich. Every year he came to Israel because he wanted to open a business there. But the taxes were too high, so he never did. Each time Jack came to Israel with his wife he would ask me to visit the United States. He would always say, "Your grandmother is getting old and you're the only grandchild left alive." I told him no every year, but in 1957 I finally said I'd go.

I decided to go to Europe first, and traveled from Israel on an Israeli ship. The first officer of the ship was a friend of mine, so I was invited to sit at his table for meals, along with an American diplomat and an English professor. The conversations were mostly in English, and my English was not all that good. Nevertheless, it was interesting.

On the Israeli ship headed for Europe

I was determined to travel through Europe and see as many countries as possible on my way to the United States. I started in Genoa, Italy, and traveled from city to city all throughout Italy. I did the same in Austria, Switzerland, and France. From Marseille, I took a boat to Dover, England, where I visited my friend Hanna, who was living in London at the time. In Liverpool, I boarded the SS Statendam, a Holland American Line ship, and set sail for America.

Just before we entered New York harbor, the ship passed by the impressive Statue of Liberty. When I saw the statue, I made a promise to myself that I would one day visit it. Eventually, I did.

Uncle Henry (the person who survived the war by going to Siberia) came to pick me up from the ship at New York harbor and took me to my grandmother Rose's apartment in Brooklyn, New York, where she lived with her husband. After I'd lived with my grandmother for some time, I was disappointed with her because every time she looked at me she would say how sad she was about her other grandchildren. There had been two other granddaughters, her daughter's children. During the war they hid in a Polish village. Someone reported them to the Germans, and when the Germans came they pulled them from their hiding place. The older of the two girls was kissing the German's boot, begging him not to kill them. As she did this, the German shot both her and her sister. Uncle Henry had learned of this after the war, and told us. Often, when I saw my grandmother, she would be crying over her lost grandchildren. I got fed up with this, thinking, "You still have one grandchild. Be happy about that." I felt like she was putting me down. What did she want from me? It was not my fault that they had died and I had survived.

My grandmother was a pretty woman. She would never admit her age, but I believe when she died she was in her late 90s. She had immigrated to the United States in the mid-1930s, because her sister lived here and had asked her to come. However, her sister died before she could reach the United States. In those days, you needed someone to pick you up when you immigrated to the United States, and if no one was there to pick you up you were sent back.

My grandmother's nephews and nieces wanted nothing to do with her, thinking she was just an old woman from some small town, Mogelnica, (which is south of Warsaw). Another cousin came, picked her up, and signed the papers for her. After grandmother had been in the United States for a number of years, her nephews and nieces finally met her, and were surprised to see such a beautiful woman. They all became her friends.

I was pretty sure my grandmother wanted to control me in some way, because she wanted me to marry some distant relative of hers. We dated a few times, and he took me to cultural places like the Metropolitan Museum and other museums, which I enjoyed. He was wealthy too, but he was short and sickly, and I'd promised myself that I would never marry a short person. The cousin who had picked my grandmother up from the ship had a granddaughter named Debbie, and she had married my husband Gerry's cousin. I met Gerry—who was six feet tall—at their wedding. When Gerry and I started talking about Israel, we found out we'd met briefly there in 1952. He had been in the US Air Force then and had taken leave to visit. I always tell people that Gerry was from another country too—because he was born in Brooklyn, New York.

When I came to the United States, I also contacted Mr. and Mrs. Zumoff, the American couple who had sponsored my mother and me in Poland after the war. My grandmother had become angry with me for not marrying her distant relative, and because of that she and Uncle Henry refused to attend my wedding to Gerry. Mr. and Mrs. Zumoff gave me away at my wedding, which was on March 1, 1958.

Our wedding was small with few people, and I didn't wear a wedding gown. After all the paperwork was finished, a rabbi wedded us in Brooklyn. We lived in Hartford, Connecticut, and on November 30, 1959, my daughter Sharon was born. My son Jesse was born there as well, on April 8, 1962. I call them "Connecticut Yankees."

I had only meant for my trip to the United States to be a visit, but after I met and married Gerry, I stayed. In

Mr. Zumoff, me, Gerry and Mrs. Zumoff

hindsight, I remember that when I'd gone to the American embassy in Tel-Aviv to get my visa, one of the American higher ups looked at me and made this prediction: "you won't be coming back." In a way she was right; though eventually our whole family moved to Israel.

Gerry's cousin worked in immigration, and he did all the paperwork for me to remain in the United States. I wanted my mother to be near us, and after Gerry's cousin did her paperwork she came to America as well. This was in 1962. She and her husband lived with us temporarily, and then they moved to Philadelphia to be near relatives.

Gerry worked for Pratt and Whitney in East Hartford, Connecticut, as a machinist in their experimental department. His particular group was involved in some of the first American missiles and space projects. He was a top-notch mechanic, and could read blueprints like we read books. Gerry worked night shifts while I worked part time in a book binding business. I was the person who embossed and gold stamped book covers before the books were bound.

In May 1967, Gamel Abdel Nasser kicked UN forces out of Sinai, and later that month he closed the Straits of Tiran to Israeli shipping. At the end of May, Egypt had signed a defense pact with Jordan and Syria. Arab nations were clearly preparing for war with Israel, and on June 4, 1967, Israel decided to attack. The following morning, Operation Focus began with a surprise Israeli airstrike on Egyptian Air Force Bases. This was the beginning of the Six-Day War.

Israel's surprise attack was extremely successful, and the Egyptian Air Force was virtually destroyed. On June 8, Israeli forces had captured Sinai. Although Jordan hadn't wanted to enter the war, Nasser convinced King Hussein that he was winning and Hussein decided to attack. Along with the Iraqis, Jordan attacked civilian settlements in Israel, and late on June 5 the Israelis launched an offensive to encircle Jerusalem. By June 7, Jerusalem had been taken by the Israelis.

The Syrians started shelling northern Israeli settlements, but Israeli aircraft attacked Syria and on June 10 Israel's final offensive was completed. After a ceasefire was signed, Israel had gained the Gaza Strip, the Sinai Peninsula, the West bank of the Jordan River (including East Jerusalem), the Golan Heights, and the city of Quneitra.

During the entire Six-Day War, Gerry and I were on pins and needles in America, hoping that everything would go well for the Israelis and that my family and friends were safe. We were ready to fly to Israel and help in any way we could, but they stopped taking volunteers. When the fighting ended, we decided that we would move to Israel. Some time after the war, we boarded a ship in New York with many Greek citizens on their way to Greece. Our ship made a stop in the Azores, Malta, and passed by Gibraltar, which we were pleased to see.

We had a cabin that didn't have a port hole, which made me feel closed in and kept me from sleeping. I complained about this, but they didn't have another cabin to offer. When we got to the Azores, however, they found a small cabin for me that happened to be over the engines. At first they hesitated to tell me about the new cabin, thinking I'd complain about the engine noise. But I enjoyed the new cabin because of two things: it had a port hole, and the hum of the engines made me sleep like a baby. We also celebrated our son Jesse's birthday on the ship.

Sharon, me and Jesse · Gerry

As our ship was closing on the shores of Israel, there was a bomb scare. All the Greeks crossed themselves and said, "Bomba, bomba!" but Gerry and I hardly paid attention to it. We were on our way to Israel. (We had visited Israel a few times previously at that time.)

My friend Varda drove a Volkswagen Bettle. During one of my visits to Israel with my children and other friends, Varda decided to take all of us to see some other friends who were living on a kibbutz. Four adults and seven children all climbed into Varda's Volkswagen, and when we arrived at the kibutz and started getting out, the people there couldn't believe what they were seeing. One by one, beginning with the children, we all climbed out of Varda's Beetle. It looked like it would never end.

Varda was waiting in Haifa when our ship docked. She took Gerry, me, and our children to a navy base, where she was stationed as a Master Sergeant, for Passover Seder. The next day, we went to a facility for new immigrants in upper Nazareth, where we were assigned a room. The facility was there for newly immigrating Jews to stay while they learned Hebrew. It happened that an American company was going to come to that area to open an aircraft parts plant, and Gerry had been offered a job with them prior to our departure from the United States.

I found out that a friend of mine, a Master Sergeant in the Israeli military police, was in charge of the city of Quneitra, Syria. I contacted him, and Gerry and I went on a private tour through the city. So I can say that I've been to Syria.

The job didn't work out for Gerry, so we decided to move. We had a friend in the Knesset, Ester Raziel-Naor, who found a beautiful, big apartment for us near Holon. Prior to this, we lived with a friend of mine in his house. I had to return to America to sell our house in Connecticut, while Gerry remained with the children in Israel.

Gerry worked at Simat, a metals technology center that specialized in sub-contracted components for metal assemblies. Simat is a subsidiary of Koor Industries. Gerry was a lathe operator at first, and later operated cutting, milling, and drilling machinery. He was highly appreciated for his work at Simat, and was involved in several high-level projects.

Because we didn't move right away into that beautiful apartment, we lost it. I sold our home in Connecticut, and while I was in America I went to visit my grandmother. She was living in Brooklyn, New York, and she was separated from her second husband. I had always felt estranged from her, but on this visit I felt like she was happy to see me. Her home needed several large repairs, including electrical. I fixed them all. My grandmother was very surprised that I was so handy and capable of doing these things, and for the first time it felt like she was glad that I was alive and well. This was the last time I saw her. She passed away when she was in her late 90s. Grandmother's life was a difficult one: her first husband died young and left her with three small children to raise. They owned a flour mill in Mogelica, Poland. She raised her children by herself, sold the flour mill, and moved to Warsaw.

When I returned to Israel we went to another facility for new immigrants, this one in Bat-Yam, where we waited for an apartment that was being built. Again, our friend Ester Raziel-Naor helped us to get the new apartment.

Gerry and I decided to open a pizzeria in Holon, so Gerry flew to the United States to purchase pizza ovens and most of the equipment we needed. We bought whatever else we needed in Israel. We found a place in one part of Holon, and we opened "Hollywood Pizza." From the very beginning, the pizza business in Holon was quite successful.

The pizzeria became so successful that people came all the way from Haifa and Jerusalem just to buy our pizzas. The lines were long and went out the door. Because of this, we hired a guy who was a Jujitsu instructor to keep people in line. We didn't have to advertise. But one of our rules was that when any of our female customers gave birth, our gift to the family was a free pizza. Gerry cooked the sauce and rolled the pizzas, and I ran the two 800-degree ovens. We didn't have air conditioning, so you can imagine how hot it got. We had four employees working full time for us. Our restaurant was closed on Fridays, which was when we'd meet with friends. When we opened the restaurant on Saturday evenings, there was no end to the long lines. Our lives in Israel were very full.

On October 6, 1973, we were sitting in our apartment in Bat-Yam, just a five-minute walk from the Mediterranean Sea, when air raid sirens started blasting in a park near us. We started hearing vehicles traveling on the roads, which never happened on Yom Kippur. We turned on the radio without knowing if there would even be a broadcast, and were surprised to hear Israeli units being called to service over the radio.

We didn't know what was happening. Later, we found out from the news: the Egyptians and Syrians had decided to attack Israel on Yom Kippur. Today, this war is known as the Yom Kippur War, the Ramadan War, the October War, or the Arab-Israeli War. I call it the Yom Kippur War, which lasted from October 6 to October 25, 1973. At the very start, hundreds of civilian cars and vehicles were mobilized for transporting troops and equipment, to include our Volkswagen.

The war was an effort by Egypt and Syria to regain territories Israel had gained during the Six-Day War and began with a massive Egyptian crossing of the Sinai. At the same time, Syria attacked the Golan Heights and made initial gains into Israeli territories. Within three days, Israeli forces had pushed the Syrians back to pre-war lines, then launched a four-day counter-offensive deep into Syria. Worried about the loss of Syria, Anwar Sadat ordered Egyptian forces to go on the offensive in the Sinai again. This offensive was quickly repulsed by the Israelis, who split Egypt's armies and crossed the Suez into Egypt. There were heavy losses on both sides during the fighting. Jordan did not participate in this war.

On October 24, 1973, after just 18 days of fierce fighting and with the Egyptian Army and the city of Suez surrounded by the Israelis, the United Nations brokered a ceasefire. But the war had come with heavy loss of life within the Israeli Defense Forces. After being heavily criticized by Israelis, in April 1974 Golda Meir, Israel's Prime Minister, stepped down.

We, the Israelis, had to pay a price for a strip of land that was rightly ours in the first place. During the War of Independence, 7,000 Israelis were killed; 1,000 more were killed in the Sinai in 1956 and 1,000 in the Six-Day War; 3,000 killed in the Yom Kippur War; many hundreds killed in various attacks by terrorists. And yet, these totals only amount to a handful of days at Auschwitz.

I am proud of being an Israeli, and my hope is that one day there will be peace there.

Because of the Yom Kippur War, Gerry decided to join the Israeli Army Reserves. Because he'd been in the US Air Force, he didn't have to attend basic training, and he wound up in a tank division. Most of his reserve time was spent on the Lebanese and Syrian borders. He was supposed to serve one month a year, but he was called up many more times than that. I had to run the pizzaria by myself when he was gone.

In 1975, my mother came to visit us from Philadelphia for my son's Bar Mitzvah, as did Uncle Henry from Brooklyn. The Bar Mitzvah was a big affair. My son was attending a private school in Israel run by Scottish nuns. All of the children of diplomats in Israel attended this school. My daughter was attending an Israeli school, but she wanted to go to the United States to complete high school. We sent her to stay with Gerry's cousin in Bloomfield, Connecticut, where she attended high school.

Though Gerry and I were doing well with our business in Israel, we didn't wish to be separated as a family. Although I was against it, we finally decided to sell the pizza business and return to the United States. We were happy to have lived to see a peace treaty signed between Israel and Egypt, and eventually between Israel and Jordan.

With two dogs and a cat, we returned to New York, where we couldn't find a place that would take animals. We eventually found a garden apartment in Valley Stream, on Long Island, close to where Uncle Henry lived. Henry asked my husband if he'd want to go into business together in a donut shop that also served breakfast and lunch, and Gerry agreed. However, the business wasn't big enough to support two families, so we sold our part to Uncle Henry.

Soon after, Gerry read about a new chain restaurant called "Wild Bill Family Restaurant," and we decided to purchase one of these restaurants in New Jersey. We moved to Netcong Heights, New Jersey, paying a lot of money for one of the franchises. After waiting a long time, and even having to threaten them, the company gave us a restaurant in Parsippany, New Jersey.

One day, people showed up at the restaurant to tell us the equipment was theirs. After some back and forth, they took almost everything. We'd been swindled, as had many others, and although we took them to court, we never received our money; the company declared bankruptcy, and we had gone broke.

Gerry finally found a job in a machine shop that built air-to-ground missiles for the US Air Force, and we remained in Netcong Heights, New Jersey. I worked as a cafeteria manager at a Hilton Hotel.

My daughter Sharon went to the University of Bridgeport, where she graduated with honors, receiving a degree of Bachelors of Fine Arts, Graphics Design and Photography, making her parents very proud. She became a member of the Sports Car Club of America, and after some time I joined as well. The following article was written in the Sports Car Club of America's newspaper:

Wanda Wolosky

During the 1981 racing season, Wanda started coming to the races. She was trying to determine why her daughter was so intrigued with flagging races . Well if you play with fire, you will eventually get singed a bit. Such is what happened. Wanda found herself working as a grid marshal and as a registrar. Wanda's enthusiasm, though apparent, is quieter than Goldilocks'. (By the way – Wanda's got the blond hair. Goldilocks is the one with the raven hair. Don't ask.) Home is Netcong, NJ. She's a manager at the Parsippany Hilton and belongs to the "Y". She drives a Matador. Wanda is married, has two children and two dogs and one cat.

Me and John Oates from the singing group
Hall and Oates

Lime Rock, Connecticut

Sharon

Paul Newman, Me and other workers

After graduating from Farleigh Dickinson University, my son Jesse went to live in Japan. At first he taught English to very wealthy Japanese people, and then he and some others started publishing the English language magazine, *Tokyo Today*. I visited him in Japan, which I really enjoyed.

Jesse and my mother at Jesse's graduation from Fairleigh Dickinson University in N.J.

Sharon

Sharon moved to Virginia to work as a civilian with the Army. They promptly sent her to Korea! As it turned out, that assignment was a gift for her, as she met her future husband, Paul, an Army Major. They had a military wedding in 1993 at Fort Myers, Virginia, which Uncle Henry and his son, Neil, were able to attend. Uncle Henry passed away one year later. In the meantime, my mother and her husband moved from Philadelphia to Netcong, New Jersey, and lived in the same garden apartments as we did.

Sharon and Paul's wedding.

My mother and Jesse

Sharon and Paul's wedding. My mother, cousin
Rahi from Israel and Jesse.

Cutting the wedding cake

Me, Sharon, Paul and Gerry

Gerry, Sharon and Baby Chance

I left my job at the Hilton after several years to work as the dining room and kitchen manager at a summer camp for senior citizens in Pennsylvania. I did this because my mother's husband had died and I wanted her to be around people her own age. By working at the camp, I could bring my mother there for the entire summer. While we were in Pennsylvania, Gerry remained in New Jersey. He would come down to see us on weekends.

We had been to Arizona a few times over the years to visit members of Gerry's family. My daughter Sharon decided to move back to the United States from her government job in Korea, and found a position at Fort Huachuca in Sierra Vista, Arizona. Gerry and I both retired, and decided to move to Arizona as well. Everything was prepared for the move when 9/11 occurred. Two days after that, my mother accidentally fell and had to be hospitalized. From there she went into a rehab center, even as we continued to prepare for our move. We had no choice but to leave her behind, as we had to close on the house we'd bought in Arizona. We traveled with our friend Lili, who had worked for me in the summer camp and who had some free time before starting a job in New York. About a month later, we sent for my mother, and she became an Arizonan as well.

My mother lived with us for some time, but when we could no longer take care of her we found a nursing facility where she could live. In 2006, less than a month before her 99th birthday, my mother passed away. She would always say that she was 100, and I would answer that she wasn't quite there yet.

I love history and have read a lot about various places, so whenever the opportunity comes up I travel to places that are interesting and exotic to me. I have visited many countries and most of the continents. No matter where I travel, I always try to learn a few words from the local language. It makes people smile and much more friendly.

I have achieved many things in my life and I am very proud of my family. Another achievement I'm very proud of is helping our troops when they are deployed overseas, risking their lives in the fight for freedom.

My Mother's Story

The following is our story as told by my mother, Blima Friedman, during an interview in the 1990s. It is not our complete story, as she was only answering questions that were posed to her during the interview. I think it's important to add my mother's thoughts on what occurred to us in Warsaw during the war, despite the fact that some of what she remembers is slightly different than what I remember.

Sharon, my daughter, has written a dedication to my mother. Her dedication is provided here as well, before my mother's story.

My Grandmother, "Bobi" Blima

by Sharon Wolosky Richwine

As a child, I remember calling her Bobi Blima our version of "Babcia" – grandma in Polish. I remember her living in Pennsylvania while we were in Connecticut, so we didn't see each other often. When she visited us, I remember she and I would take walks around the neighborhood and pick apples off a neighbor's tree. When we visited her, I remember her taking me to the dress shop that she worked at. She was responsible for most if not all the bead/sequins work done on the evening gowns. I remember being amazed at the amount of work that goes into transforming a somewhat simple dress into an elegant evening gown, and my grandmother did that. She showed me the stiches and explained the passion and patient needed to get it right.

As an adult, I saw my grandmother in another light. Since my childhood, she had moved closer to my parents in New Jersey, living two-apartment buildings away from them. Although close, she kept her distance unless she needed help or it was time to take her shopping. I remember, she cooked simple food but boy was her chicken soup with matzo balls to die for, so was her homemade kreplach (Jewish version of a tortellini). She would take numerous walks throughout the apartment complex, and knew everything that was going on there. She was never silent about her opinions; although she wasn't pushy about it, unless it was focused about the family. My father, would often argue with her, and say she was a pain, but when she wasn't around he would always voice his love and respect for her.

I'm unsure of when she finally told me about her experience during the war. She would provide little bits here and there of what she and my mother went through. She never held ill will against the Germans and always reminded me that there were good and bad people in every nationality. My grandmother focused more on now and me. As the first to go and graduate college, she was so proud. When she met my husband, Paul, she checked him out and took him at face value and was the first to accept him into the family. Years later, when she met my son Chance at three months old it was like they had a common language. Both taking turns making baby sounds. Although she didn't have the closeness to her two great granddaughters (Jade and Lin), she loved them as well.

In the last months of her life, she would tell me that she's lived a long life and got to see both grandchildren grow up and have three great grandchildren. She was ready for God to take her. Even with the oncoming of dementia, she had moments of humor, when telling me that she doesn't speak English, only Polish; all the while saying this to me in English and understanding my responses to her in English because I don't speak any Polish. Since her passing, I often think about her and what she like so many others went through and wonder why? Grandma, if you hear me, I hope I've made you proud and love you.

Loving Granddaughter

My Mother's Story

I was born on September 15, 1907, in Warsaw, Poland. We lived on Krochmalna Street, across from Janusz Korczak's orphanage. My father, Jakow Szturman, was a tailor in Warsaw. My mother was Gitl Polick. I was the third of six children. Two of my brothers and sisters died rather young, prior to World War I. I don't remember when the others died. This left only my older brother Mordechai and me.

When my sister and I went to pre-school, our father would walk with us and come to pick us up. There were rumors that gypsies would snatch children, and we were both beautiful girls. One of my older brothers was a very gifted child, and Janusz Korczak would come to our house and take him to summer camp. This brother died early in life.

During World War I, and after my mother passed away, my father decided to take us out of Warsaw to his mother's home. On the way there, the Germans captured us in a town whose name I can't remember and put us in a jail that was full of rats. My father told a German officer that we were going to his mother's house in Tyszowce. The officer told us we weren't allowed to go there, and that we'd have to return to Warsaw. After we were released from jail, instead of returning to Warsaw, my father asked a Jewish group to help him, and they lent him a horse and buggy to drive us to the city of Lublin, where we had family. From there we went to Zamoscz. We eventually made it to my grandmother's house in Tyszowce. When people in the area found out my father was a tailor from Warsaw, he got a lot of work. Even a Protestant minister (who had come from Austria) came to have his clothing tailored. After World War I ended, father returned alone to Warsaw to see what was happening there. When he came back, all of us went back with him to Warsaw. My father then remarried. He married my mother's sister, Rezza Polick, and they had two sons: Aron, who died in a concentration camp in 1940, and Zelig, who died in the Warsaw Ghetto in 1943.

When I finished school, I wanted to go on to a vocational school to learn a trade. We had a relative who was a manicurist, and she told me I could make good money doing that. So I became one, and was very famous for it. A doctor, one of my clients, asked me why I didn't also do pedicures, so I started doing this as well.

I married Avram Leib Milsztajn in 1932, and we lived with my father. My husband, along with a friend, eventually opened a wholesale meat business. My first child, a boy, died just after he was born. After some time, my daughter was born. I used to call her Gutka as a nickname. Much later she would change her name to Wanda, but that's her story. My father loved me and my daughter very much. Sadly, he died of cancer in 1938.

By then there had been a lot of talk of war, and in September 1939, Germany invaded Poland. They didn't invade Warsaw initially, and when the German airplanes first appeared over the city, we thought they were part of the Polish Air Force. During that time, I was on duty every night from midnight to 2 am with one other person. Our job was to ensure people went into basements when German airplanes flew over the city. Every apartment building was set up this way, with people standing guard for the same reason.

When we went into the basement, my daughter would cry because she was hungry and there was no food, not even bread. There was also a shortage of water because the Germans had bombed the water pipes. Bombs hit one section of our building and a woman was killed.

Four weeks after the invasion of Poland, the Germans finally entered Warsaw. They took men to clean the streets and fix the trams (streetcars) that had been turned over. They gave flour to bakeries to bake bread because everyone was hungry. When I went to the bakery, the line was so long that I thought I wouldn't get any bread. So I picked up my daughter and walked to the beginning of the line, where there was an SS guard watching people. He gave me one loaf of bread and another to my daughter. Everyone watching was surprised. Standing in the line was a woman from our building who always called me "that Jew woman." When she saw me with the bread, she said, "Look at that Jew woman. She has two loaves of bread. By the time it's my turn there won't be any bread left." So I gave her one of our loaves. She didn't know what to say.

We also needed water, and though they opened the street faucets, people still had to stand in line and wait their turn to be able to fill their basin or bucket.

My husband and his brother, along with many other men, decided to go to Bialystok, a city in Poland that was under Russian control at that time. I didn't want to go because I knew that Russia was a very cold country, and I had a small child to care for. My sister-in-law went to Bialystok to be with her husband, my husband's brother, but in 1940 she returned because she had an apartment in Warsaw. By then, the Germans had already created the Warsaw Ghetto.

On Yom Kippur in 1940, we went to synagogue, and when we came out there were posters all over announcing that the Germans were creating the ghetto. We needed to move there, and I tried to go to Wronia Street, which was going to be a part of the ghetto. But when the Germans decided that Wronia Street wouldn't be part of the ghetto, we had to return to our apartment. Eventually, I found a place on Nowolipki Street where a single woman was living, and we exchanged apartments.

Soon after, many of the men who had gone to Bialystok returned to the Warsaw Ghetto. One of the men who returned told me that the Germans had caught my husband on his way back to Warsaw and killed him. My brother-in-law survived by going to Russia.

Somehow my husband's mother, Rose Milsztajn, who lived in Brooklyn, NY, was able to send some money to us through a bank. The bank that the money was sent to was on the Aryan side, so we got dressed in some very elegant clothes and jumped on a tram that went through the streets of the ghetto. At first none of the bank tellers could figure out how these two Jews got out of the ghetto. I figured we'd either starve to death or get shot, so, knowing my options, I wasn't really afraid. I told my daughter to make sure she survived, because she had a grandmother in the United States. We returned to the ghetto the same way we left, but this time with our money. I decided to use some of the money to have good shoes made for my daughter and me to get us through the cold winters.

When we left our apartment for the ghetto, our building caretaker told me we could stay with him and his wife, but we decided to leave. By December, I decided to leave the ghetto with my daughter. At the ghetto's gates, there was a German soldier with a gun, a Polish and a Jewish policeman both with rubber truncheons (a type of club). Because we were always nicely dressed, I decided to try and tell them that I wanted to go to the Aryan side to get potatoes, because I had coupons. We had to wait a long time, and my daughter began to cry because it was very cold. The Jewish and Polish policemen said that the German was a good person, so I told my daughter to cry even louder. The German soldier asked why my daughter was crying and I told him it was because she was cold and we wanted to go to the Polish side for potatoes. He actually let us go.

We returned to our old building and stayed overnight with our caretaker. I needed money to buy food. In the morning, he told me not to go to the ghetto yet, but to stay with them. It was just before Christmas, and the caretaker and his wife told me to leave my daughter with them so I could do manicures for my previous clients. We stayed with them for a couple of weeks, then went back to the ghetto.

They were only giving people in the ghetto one-fourth of a loaf of bread for two days, and one frozen rutabaga, which no one could eat. When you got your bread, you needed to hide it under your coat because young boys would take it from you and throw it into sewage so you didn't want it. They would still eat it. I would give my daughter a small piece of bread, take a little for myself, and hide the rest.

I needed food, and the only way to get it was to get out of the ghetto. One way to get out of the ghetto was through the basements. Some of the buildings were bombed, so you could go from one side to the other through a basement. You could also go through the sewage system or through the Jewish cemetery on Gensia Street, because the other side of the cemetery was the Catholic portion, and it was not in the ghetto. Any time I left I took my daughter with me.

One time, while we were standing near a headstone in the cemetery, my daughter said she had to go to the bathroom. I told her to go near another headstone to do it. A German soldier spotted us and came over to ask what we were doing. I said that my daughter had to go to the bathroom. Luckily, he left us. The Germans patrolled the cemeteries all the time.

We would go out of the ghetto and stay on the Polish side for two or three days, sleeping wherever we could, mostly in our old caretaker's apartment. Eventually, someone saw me go to the caretaker's place, and said if I returned they'd turn me in for a reward. So I couldn't go there anymore. We sometimes stayed with my clients, and once we went to a woman who was our neighbor, who let us sleep on her kitchen floor. Her son came home and saw us and started screaming at her for allowing us to stay. So, needless to say, we couldn't stay there anymore. After that, we returned to the ghetto.

When we were going in and out of the ghetto, I had to keep the Jewish armband I was forced to wear. I would cover it with a shawl, or just take it off so I didn't advertise that I was Jewish. If they had caught me without the star, the punishment would have been immediate execution.

The next time we left the ghetto, I decided that we wouldn't go back. We slept under stairs and in basements, and one day, as we were walking, the woman from my old building who called me "that Jew woman" saw us. She asked us what we were doing there, and I told her we needed somewhere to stay. You never knew who was your friend or enemy, because they could take you to the police station where you got shot and they got paid for being good citizens. She told me to follow her.

She took us to the cemetery, where she had an office. She was the person in charge of taking orders for headstones. We stayed there for a few weeks, and every morning she would bring food and share it with us. During the day, we had heat from a little stove, but at night we were freezing.

After some time, I found a place for us to stay with a woman I knew and her son, who lived across from a convent that was responsible for saving many Jews. She also rented a bed to another man, who didn't know we were Jewish. When we stayed with her, I worked in a restaurant that one of my clients owned.

I hurt my finger at work one day, and gangrene soon set in. I had to return to the ghetto to see a doctor, who performed surgery to take off a part of my finger. Luck was with me, as I was able to escape from the ghetto once again.

Sometimes, my younger brother would leave the ghetto under German guard with groups of men in work parties, and we would go to the gate of the ghetto to try to sneak him some food. But after a while, we stopped seeing him. I never saw him again and to this day I don't know what happened to him.

On Palm Sunday, 1943, the first day of Passover, the Warsaw Ghetto uprising began. All this time, while the ghetto was burning, I worked cleaning people's homes. When I walked the streets of Warsaw, I tried to cover my face to make sure nobody would recognize me. After the Germans burned the ghetto, they gave orders that if a Jew was found hiding, everyone else in that building would also be shot.

Everything was so crazy, I wasn't sure where we would end up. There was a man in the building where we were hiding who was willing to take the bounty money for giving up Jews. One day his wife saw us. She knew we were Jewish, so we decided that we had to leave in case she told her husband.

Someone suggested we go to the convent, but I didn't want to go there because we would have had to convert to Christianity. I decided to send my daughter to see a woman who lived one floor above the person who owned the restaurant where I worked. My daughter went, and the woman told her to go back and bring me with her. She said we could live with her because she didn't want to live alone during these uncertain times. She didn't know that we were Jewish.

One day, the woman's brother brought a man to stay in the same apartment. My daughter came to me later and said that she heard the man counting in Yiddish. At first I didn't believe her, but she was sure of what she was saying, that he was counting in Yiddish. I finally went to him and told him, "you can't stay here." When he asked why, I told him, "Because you're Jewish, and so am I." He was stunned, because I was speaking to him in perfect Polish.

When my daughter saw children playing, I had to keep her away from them so that no one knew we were Jewish. I worked and made some money, and we had it good outside the ghetto. We could wash ourselves and our clothes, and we had sufficient amounts of food. One day, at work, someone told me I should leave because something was about to happen. That was the day the Polish uprising began.

As I walked home, I saw many Germans with guns and there was a lot of shooting. I had to walk close to the buildings to get home. The woman we lived with couldn't come home for two days because of the uprising. She was a cook for a family and just stayed with them. My daughter and I sat in a basement for a number of days. When the Germans came back to the city, they took all the men out of hiding and killed them. They came to our building on the seventh day, which was the day they stopped shooting civilians. The Germans threw a hand grenade down the steps, yelling for everyone in the basement to get out. I told my daughter we couldn't leave, because we didn't have identification papers. A few minutes later, a man came to tell us in Polish to leave because the Germans were about to burn the building. My daughter kicked at the door until it opened, and we left. I didn't want to leave because we were told the Germans were swinging children by their legs and bashing their heads against the buildings. As we left, some of the buildings on both sides of the street were on fire and there were dead bodies strewn along the sidewalks.

At one point, there was a German patrol in the middle of the street checking papers, which we didn't have. My daughter started jumping up and down saying she had to go to the bathroom. A German soldier told us to go into one of the nearby buildings and we managed to get around the patrol. We kept walking with all the people who'd had their papers checked and were put into a big church. In the church, I saw people from our old neighborhood, but they didn't say anything about us being Jewish. There was only one German, actually half German and half Polish, in the church, and he was mad because he wanted to go home and couldn't because of the uprising. He was commonly known as the Volksdeutsche. If anyone came close to him he'd hit them with the butt of his gun.

The Volksdeutsche received an order from his superiors to move people, so he asked if anyone wanted to go. He said if they wanted to leave for this new place they could, but they didn't have to go if they didn't want to. I didn't know what to do because we didn't know where they were taking us and I didn't want them to take my daughter. The woman we'd been staying with was there as well, but she'd been wounded and couldn't go anywhere. Each time I looked, more and more people had left the church, so I sent my daughter to ask if we should go as well. The Volksdeutsche patted her on her head and told her we should leave right away, because today the march would be slow and the following days it would be worse. I went and told him that the big gate to the church was closed, but he came and he opened it for us. We were able to leave, not knowing where we were going.

It was the first of August, and hot, so we had our winter coats over our arms. We walked until we made it to a small town called Piastow, where there was a rubber factory. There were lots of German and Polish people on the streets asking what was going on. One of the Poles, a woman, told me she wanted to take my daughter to her house. I said, "What about me? Am I a dog?" The woman told me that if I could get around the line of people watching, she would take me in as well. The people in the line made room for us to pass and we went into the factory office. Inside, they asked me what was going on in Warsaw, but since I didn't know who they were I just said that the Poles in the city had taken part in an uprising.

While we were in the office, the woman who promised to take us in disappeared. A German officer came and asked us if we had somewhere to go and I told him about the woman just as she was returning. The German didn't want us to go through the factory's front door, so he took us all the way to the back of the factory and let us out a door that was almost where the woman lived.

When we went to her home, we had to wait outside because the woman's sister had the key to her room. As we waited, a Ukrainian on a big horse rode up and asked if we knew of any bandits from Warsaw that were in the area. We told him no, and he left.

It turned out that when we left the church, we were supposed to have gone to the village of Pruszkow, where there was a transition camp. From there, the Germans were sending people to various other concentration camps.

Half of the rubber factory in Piastow had been converted to a hospital for the wounded. My daughter would go to the hospital and bring food back for us. Then she said that she wanted to sell cigarettes at the hospital, so we made a little box with a string around her neck so she could keep the cigarettes in it.

One day, a German tank battalion came into the town. They were looking for people to peel potatoes, so I went to work for them in their kitchen. A German named Herman told me one day to wash a very big and dirty pot, so I cleaned it so good that it shined. When all the women and I were eating he told me to make sure my daughter came to eat as well. A Babushka (an older woman) who was living around the corner came and told me her children had nothing to eat. I gave her a few potatoes to hide in her pockets, and told her to come back for more.

One time, a wounded German soldier arrived. For some reason he couldn't eat black bread, and I had some white bread I'd bought. I told Herman to give him the white bread, and the Germans there were amazed that I'd helped their fellow soldier. Later, they asked me to clean their rooms. Eventually, a high ranking officer asked who was doing such a good job cleaning, and that he wanted that person to clean his room. I did such a good job that the officer gave me a pass that showed I worked for the Germans. Because of that pass, I now had papers I could show any German who stopped me. After the war, I tore the pass to pieces.

A woman came to the German tank division kitchen one day and told the Babushka that I was Jewish. The Babushka said, "What are you talking about? I've known her for a long time from Warsaw, and she's not Jewish." The woman kept quiet after that. When I went shopping for bread, the same woman stopped me, and I remembered that one night I slept in her house. When she approached me, I told her "I wish there was a big hole I could fall into. I don't understand why people are so jealous that I'm alive." She told me that her husband was very sick and had nothing to eat, so I gave her half of the bread I had to shut her up.

In January 1945, when the Russians liberated Piastów, I stopped one of the soldiers to talk to him. He was tall and wearing a long Russian overcoat. He told me they'd marched all the way from Lvov and that his whole family had been killed. I figured maybe he was Jewish, so I asked him. He said he was, and I told him I was Jewish as well. I asked him what I should do. He told me to sit quietly and don't do or say anything. He said that they were on their way to Berlin.

I saw more and more Russian soldiers coming. I saw one of them wearing a Russian hat and told him I was from Warsaw, asking where he was from. He said he was from Warsaw too, that he was Jewish. He told me that if I wanted to find out if someone was Jewish during a conversation I should say "Amhu," the Hebrew word for "His People." If the person is Jewish they'll answer, and if they're not they'll ask me what I said and I can say, "Oh, nothing." I took over my daughter's business selling cigarettes and Russian newspapers to the Russians.

That's what I started doing with all of the soldiers, saying "Amhu" when I spoke to them. This is how I met a Jewish captain and other Jewish officers in the Russian army. After that, they'd ask me what they could do for me. I'd tell them that we needed a place of our own to stay, and that we'd been sleeping on the floor. They told me to find a room, and they assured me I'd get one.

I found a room in a three-room villa, then went back and told the Russians I needed a bed. A Russian captain asked me why I hadn't gone to him in the first place, that he would have gotten me whatever I needed, and he said he didn't know I was Jewish. All of the Jewish Russian officers were happy to have found a Jewish woman with a child.

I'd overheard people talking about an office for Jewish matters opening in Warsaw. It was in the Praga district which is on the east bank of the Vistula River. I went there and gave them my information. In the meantime, my mother-in-law Rose Milsztajn (Milstein) from the United States was searching for us, and my brother-in-law returned from Russia. He found our names from the information I'd given the committee, and came to Piastów to see us. We went to the Jewish Committee to get food, but the people in charge were Russian and wouldn't let us have any. I got angry with them and told them that I'd suffered enough hunger in the Ghetto, and if they didn't want me telling everyone they were selling the food on the "Black Market" they better give me some. I got the food.

My daughter got sick, so I took her to a doctor in Warsaw who told us the problem was where we were living.

The doctor decided my daughter needed to live in a drier climate than the area we lived in now. So I took her to a sanatorium at Dolny Śląsk and returned to Piastów. My daughter spent over a year in the sanatorium. Someone took her to Lodz after that year, and I went to Lodz to pick her up. Instead of returning with her to Piastów, I left her instead in a city Kibbutz for several months. The Kibbutz decided to leave Poland for Palestine in 1947, so I took Wanda to an orphanage in Otwock that also took in children with single parents who couldn't care for their children. Since I was working, I had to pay for my daughter to stay in the orphanage.

We decided to go to Israel. The first group of Polish Jews left for Israel in 1949. Ours was the second group. We needed to get passports to leave, and to get our passports we had to sign affidavits stating that we were no longer citizens of Poland. We left Warsaw at the beginning of May, 1950, and traveled through Czechoslovakia, Austria, and Italy. We boarded a ship in Genoa, Italy, and arrived in Israel five or six days later.

I knew I had an aunt in Israel, my father's sister, and I tried to find her there. I eventually did, and found out that I had other family members in Israel as well.

Life was difficult in Israel at that time. It was a new country and there were constant battles with our Arab neighbors. My daughter and I stayed with my cousin Rachel Ball and her son Dovik for awhile. Through some friends, I met and married Dov Friedman, partly because he had an apartment we could move into.

My daughter Wanda volunteered to join the Israeli Army when she was 17. When she was honorably discharged from the Army, she went on vacation to America, but got married and stayed. Five years later, in 1962, my husband and I moved to the United States as well. First we stayed with Wanda and her husband Gerry in Connecticut, before moving to Philadelphia where I became a seamstress at a local formal gown store. I did very elegant bead and lace work. To be closer to family, my husband and I moved to Long Island when Wanda and her family moved there. Finally we moved to Netcong, New Jersey where my husband died.

Wanda and her mother in Green Valley, Arizona

The History of the Warsaw Ghetto

Approximately 360,000 Jews lived in Warsaw in 1939. When the Warsaw Ghetto was created, that number had reached 500,000, meaning that each square kilometer of the ghetto contained approximately 128,000 Jews. The Warsaw Ghetto was in fact the largest prison in Europe, with 500,000 Jews packed into approximately 100 acres.

September 1939

Germany conquered western Poland, and in accordance with the terms of a Nazi-Soviet Non-Aggression Treaty, eastern Poland was annexed into the Soviet Union. When Germany launched its Blitzkrieg (lightning war) against Poland, England and France—who'd made a pact with Poland—declared war on Germany. The German attack came from the air and on land. On the first day of the war, the orphanage at Otwock was hit (I lived in this orphanage after the war).

Warsaw, the capital of Poland, woke to a new reality. The Polish government withdrew from the capital, and in radio broadcasts it called for all military-aged men to leave the city and assemble near the Bug River. Tens of thousand of Jews were drafted into the Polish Army, and thousands of them died in battle for their country. Thousands more were captured.

The German Air Force did not differentiate between military and civilian targets and bombed populated areas repeatedly. They'd prepared six years for this moment, by the way. They used two types of bombs: one demolished buildings and the other burned them down. Twenty percent of Warsaw was destroyed. The water lines were destroyed. Important cultural buildings were destroyed.

There are just two things a person really cares about: their life, and a loaf of bread. But the city ran out of flour, and the bakers did not have enough to bake their bread. And still the bombing continued.

Street after street was destroyed, especially in the Jewish areas in the city. Entire families were buried beneath the rubble. Perhaps this was deliberately done on the holiest of days for Jews—Rosh Hashanah (New Year) and Yom Kippur (The Day of Atonement). The

German war planes over Poland, September 1939

city was defeated, its roads overflowing with refugees fleeing the city and others who were poring into the city from areas of the country already occupied by the Germans. They were all prime targets for German pilots, who killed thousands on the roads by flying in low.

The Germans were cutting off all approaches to the city, bombing bridges, railway tracks, roads, flying very low and strafing the helpless masses. At the start of the war, the Poles drew closer to the Jews. They seemed almost eager to forget their hatred. For their part, the Jews were relieved, hoping that maybe they wouldn't have to face the enemy alone.

On September 7, 1939, Nazi forces reached the outskirts of Warsaw, laying seige to the city. The city had prepared for the invasion, its citizens taking part in digging trenches and building barricades. The people somehow believed this would stop the onslaught, but Warsaw was not ready for a long siege. They continued to shell the city with artillery and aerial bombs all day and night. The whole city was in flames.

The partnership between Jews and Poles ended, with the Jews again being blamed for the war and all the suffering. Gangs of Polish youths broke into Jewish stores and looted them. They chased after Jews, robbed and assaulted them. For Jews, there was no protection. There was no effective police force. Merchants lost everything, but nobody cared. The bombs were still falling on the city when news came on September 29 that the Polish Army had been defeated. Warsaw had suffered the heaviest shelling, and the

Germans gladly accepted its surrender.

A silence fell across the battered, beaten city. German cruelty spread through the streets long before the Nazi forces were there, as rumors had arrived with Jewish refugees who searched for safety in Warsaw. Europe was again at war with Germany, this time with the Nazis.

In the meantime, 360,000 Warsaw Jews were caught in the claws of the Nazis, completely unsure of their futures.

October 1939

The day after Warsaw surrendered, the Germans created bread distribution centers for the starving residents. As proof of their "generosity," they took photographs of the long lines of hungry and weak residents receiving food. The so-called friendship between the Poles and the Jews had ended even before the Germans entered the city, and now that relationship became even worse. Jews tried to join in on the food lines, but they were told: "No food for the Jew."

A true hatred for the Jews now became vicious. If a Jew tried to stand in a food line, shouts of "Jude, Jude!" would rise up, and the only thing they would get was kicked and their beards yanked. The Poles returned to full-scale pogroms against the Jews, and this was only the beginning. It became an opportunity for German soldiers and officers (one they didn't actually need) to show their own cruelty. They never missed an opportunity to torment the Jews. The endless number of decrees they issued began to exclude the Jews from society more and more, without rights or safeguards, until the Jews were being treated like animals.

In early October, Hitler came to Warsaw to view his victorious forces as they marched in their victory parade. On October 15, 1939, 24 Jewish males were appointed to the Council of Elders, the *Judenrat*. The council was responsible for implementing all of the orders the Germans gave them. If the orders were not obeyed, the council would be severely punished. Czerniakow was the head of this council, and he and the other *Judenrat* became servants of the German regime. Bribery quickly became an accepted part of the *Judenrat* and its enforcement arm, the Jewish police.

Jewish policemen carried clubs and wore black boots and uniforms. They wore long raincoats and special caps. They were responsible for assembling and escorting their fellow Jews to various locations to be used as forced labor. Once the ghetto was established, they were responsible for internal security and guarding the ghetto gates. They also became responsible for evacuating Jews from the neighboring towns and relocating them to the city. The reason for this, they were told, was that Jews were taking part in partisan activities (guerrilla fighters).

On September 21, 1939, just prior to Warsaw's capitulation to the Germans, Hans Frank, the designated Governor of Poland, met secretly in Berlin with Reinhard Heydrich, a Gestapo leader. The meeting concerned "the Jewish problem." From that meeting, a protocol was issued "to gather all of the Jews residing in the suburbs into the large cities." This was to be done quickly, and only in cities that served as railway crossroads or were close to rail lines.

The Nazis wasted no time in immediately implementing decrees designed to make life miserable for Jews. The following is a list of just the first decrees issued by the Germans in 1939 and 1940. The list grew more stringent as time passed:

Oct 12, 1939: Jews cannot withdraw deposits, securities, cash or gold from the banks and are limited to withdrawals of 200 zlotys per week. A Jewish family cannot possess more than 2,000 zloty in cash.

Oct 21, 1939: Jews may not deal in textiles and processed leathers.

Oct 22, 1939: Jews may not own radios or enter movie theaters.
Jewish teachers may not teach in Polish schools.

Nov 15, 1939: Jewish women may not engage in prostitution.

Nov 17, 1939: A curfew imposed on all Jews in Warsaw from five o'clock in the evening until eight o'clock the following morning.

Dec 1, 1939: Jews from the age of 12 must wear an armband with a blue Star of David. A Star of David must be pasted on all Jewish-owned stores.

Dec 3, 1939: Jews may not enter the central post office.

Dec 5, 1939: All Jewish schools and educational institutions are closed.

Dec 22, 1939: Jews may not use Polish passports and may not own telephones.

Dec 23, 1939: All Jews must declare all the property in their possession or ownership.

Jan 14, 1940: All Jews between the ages of 12 and 60 are sent to camps for re-education.

Jan 24, 1940: All synagogues and houses of worship in Warsaw are closed.

Feb 10, 1940: Jews may not travel by train between cities in Poland.

Apr 7, 1940: Jews may not open bookstores.

Jul 6, 1940: Jews may not mail letters abroad.

Jul 8, 1940: All Jewish-owned printing shops are closed.

Jul 29, 1940: Jews may not enter parks, municipal areas and specified streets in the center of Warsaw and may not sit on public benches.

Aug 22, 1940: Jewish peddlers and merchants may not purchase goods in neighboring villages.

Aug 27, 1940: Jews may not own bakeries or coaches.

Aug 29, 1940: Jews may not buy a German book.

Sep 6, 1940: Pilsudski Square is renamed Hitler Square and is off-limits to Jews.

Sep 19, 1940: Jewish doctors may not treat Polish patients and Polish doctors may not treat Jewish patients.

Sep 25, 1940: Jews may only ride in trolleys bearing the Star of David.

Oct 4, 1940: Polish maids may not work in Jewish homes.

Oct 31, 1940: A monthly tax of five zlotys is imposed on Jews using trolleys.

Nov 15, 1940: All Jews in Warsaw are transferred to the ghetto.

Nov 19, 1940: All Jewish property found outside the ghetto walls is confiscated.

But the Nazis didn't just confiscate money; they took gold and silver as well. They coveted Jewish homes, entered them with pistols drawn and took whatever they wanted: furniture, appliances, paintings and other valuables. They murdered anyone who resisted, or punished them mercilessly. Sometimes the money satisfied them, and other times they beat and tortured babies, pregnant women, and the elderly. Jews were forced to take their belongings to the streets and pay for transport. They were beaten, whipped, and screamed at. Jews were frightened. Mothers were told, "Jewish children don't need beds or blankets. They can sleep on the floor and you can cover them with old newspapers."

Time passed, and the situation grew worse. The Wehrmacht was replaced by the merciless Einsatzgruppen and the special security police that were under direct command of the Gestapo.

On October 25, 1939, Dr. Hans Frank was appointed as the new governor of Poland. This signaled a new period of uncertainty and danger for the Jews. German troops would walk the streets searching out Jews with beards, and when they found them they would tear at and cut off their beards. Young and old, men and women were taken from the streets, beaten, humiliated, and sent to be used as forced labor.

Doctors, lawyers, and businessmen were forced to polish tiles with toothbrushes at the city center. Others were made to sing and dance at gunpoint. Hundreds were taken to the city squares and forced to perform military exercises, or to crawl through the streets and run back and forth, all the while being beaten and whipped.

Jewish women were publicly humiliated, forced to undress in the streets and undergo body searches. The Germans took their jewelry, fur coats, and abused them sexually. They searched their breasts and private parts, and if the woman's family was there they forced their husbands and children to watch. If you protested, you were beaten.

They search the woman's private body parts, forcing her husband and children to watch

The fear was everywhere; you weren't safe at home, on the streets, or at work. Jews were humiliated in food lines. When a Jew forgot to clear the way for a German on the sidewalk, he or she was beaten until they were unconcious. One Jew, sent to clean the German army's cesspool, was beaten simply for asking for rags. "Use your coat," they told him, then forced him to enter the latrines naked and use his own clothes for rags. After hours of cleaning, without food or water, he was forced to wear his soiled clothes and run home barefoot.

A Rabbi was forced to spit on the Torah scrolls. When his mouth became dry, a German spat into the Rabbi's mouth and forced him to continue at gunpoint. Another Jew was forced to transfer blocks of ice from one place to another with his bare hands in subzero temperatures. His hands became frostbitten and had to be amputated.

Many Jews hoped that all of this would pass, thinking that Germany was a civilized nation. It was the cradle of European civilization, after all. None could know, of course, that the worst was yet to come.

Slowly but surely, Jews were expelled from all professions. There was no more work in the textile and leather sectors for Jews. Merchants, brokers, shoemakers, store owners, teachers, university professors, printers...all were suddenly unemployed. Jewish coach owners were not allowed to own horses, and Jewish doctors were only allowed to treat Jewish patients.

With no income and no money, Jews received vouchers that bore the Star of David. Hunger was the norm, and then starvation set in.

The Germans rationed daily portions of food according to race. The pure breeds—Germans and Poles of German origin—were entitled to almost unlimited food at absurdly low prices: 2,613 calories per person per day at .3 zloty per calorie (784 zloty). Poles could receive one third that amount, 654 calories, at 2.6 zloty per calorie per day (1,700 zloty). Jews were authorized a mere 184 calories a day at 5.6 zloty per calorie (1,030 zloty).

When food was available, Jews could receive 80 grams of bread (about two slices), several potatoes, a few grams of sugar, less than ten grams of jam, and a dash of salt. On those rations, survival was impossible. A post-war study concluded that the ghetto would have ceased to exist within five years on that kind of diet, even if the Germans hadn't sent the ghetto Jews to Treblinka gas chambers.

Self-aid centers were established in Jewish buildings, where thin slices of bread and bowls of watery soup were given out. Many thousands were helped at these centers, which saved many lives (for a short time, of course). And then came the winter of 1939, one of the harshest since the turn of the century.

Temperatures that winter fell to minus 20 degrees Farenheit, and sometimes lower. The Jews endured freezing weather during the long hours of curfew. There was no coal to heat Jewish homes, no blankets or extra clothing that hadn't already been stolen by the Germans or Poles, and there was no money. Still, all of this was oveshadowed by the unbearable hunger, the starvation.

It was then that the Germans began to expel Jews from the neighboring towns into Warsaw. They were given so little time to pack that they were forced to leave most of their belongings behind. On December 1, 1939, Jews were forced to wear the Star of David armband, a blue star upon a white background, on their right arms. Jewish children in Warsaw 12 and over wore the armbands, and from 10-12 they wore them in other places. Jewish curfew was one hour longer than for other residents.

Jews were prohibited from being in the city parks, in the streets, and in the squares. They were thrown off trains designated for Poles only, and from any trolley that didn't specifically bear the Star of David (designating it as a Jewish trolley). If you dared breach any of these decrees, your punishment was death.

A trolley in the Warsaw streets. Cars for Jews only.

The first executions included 53 men. Two months later, 225 were executed. And still, despite the murders, humiliation, plundering, and all of the decrees, most Jews continued to believe that they would somehow survive the German occupation.

January 1940

On January 18, 1940, a senior Nazi official arrived in Warsaw with a letter of authority to plan the creation of the ghetto. Their reasoning for the ghetto was that it would protect German soldiers from being infected with diseases that the Jews carried, to end the problem of black market trading, and to separate the Jews and the Poles. But of course there were political considerations.

On March 27, 1940, the Gestapo ordered the Jews to begin building a wall around the designated ghetto area immediately, and to pay for it themselves. Bricks for the ghetto walls were taken from destroyed buildings and sold to the Jews. Construction of the wall continued until the end of October. Jews were forced to collect money and pay for hundreds of thousands of glass bottles, which were then broken and placed on top of the 12-mile long, 11.5-foot high wall. The glass was placed there to prevent Jews from climbing the wall to get to the other side. In some places, barbed wire was used. Once the wall was finished, signs were put up immediately in German and Polish, that read "No Entry—Disease Infected Area," and "Typhus."

Bad news, it seemed, always came on Jewish holy days. That Yom Kippur, loud speakers throughout Warsaw announced: "All Jews must relocate to the ghetto by October 31." They'd given the 150,000 Jews that lived outside the ghetto just three days to move inside the walls. The order was signed by Hans Frank, the governor. After that, any Jew found outside the ghetto without permission would be executed.

The *Judenrat* appealed the order to the military governor, who despised the Gestapo and SS. He was able to postpone the date for a few weeks, which the Germans agreed to. On November 1, 1940, the Germans announced that the deadline for moving into the ghetto was in two-weeks time, but not a day longer.

The gates to the Warsaw Ghetto were closed on November 16, 1940. At first, the Germans were somewhat lenient towards Jews who violated the orders, but on November 23 a new edict was issued proclaiming that any Jew who left the ghetto without permission would be killed. Some didn't believe it, but the proof was not long in coming when six men and two women were caught smuggling bread and potatoes. They were led to prison and executed.

Once the 13 gates were closed, communcation with the outside world was closed as well. The only communication that occurred came in the form of rumors supplied by the Germans. No one was allowed in or out of the ghetto without permission. All Jewish businesses remaining on the Aryan side of the ghetto were confiscated and transferred to Germans, or Poles of German origin (*Voksdeutche*).

The Germans ruled the ghetto with an iron fist, they were the lords of life and death. They ordered the Jewish Council (the *Judenrat*) and the Jewish police to do their dirty work inside the ghetto. The Jewish police force was 1,700 strong. At first, along with the Polish police and the Germans, the Jewish police guarded the ghetto gates. Their primary duty was to patrol the borders of the ghetto and to keep order inside its walls. At first, Jews welcomed them, but by the spring of 1941 they had become the enemy. They captured child-smugglers and handed them over to the Germans to be shot. They participated in brutal roundups. They later took part in escorting Jews to the train station, where they were loaded into cattle cars bound for the Treblinka Death Camp.

111

If hell could be described in just three words, those words would be "The Warsaw Ghetto." Behind the walls and gates, about 500,000 Jews lived in a diabolical state of starvation, murder, fear, loss and hopelessness. The ghetto was a hellish place where life had no meaning. You were lucky that the haggard body lying dead in the street wasn't you, and that the child shot as he or she tried to smuggle food wasn't your child. **The ghetto was an industry of death.**

The children suffered the most. There were approximately 100,000 children in the ghetto, 75,000 of whom suffered hunger from the very first day. They could be found crowded around garbage, searching for leftover food or potato peels. Most were barefoot and so swollen from hunger that it was impossible for them to move. Some begged for a slice of bread, or simply lay helplessly on the sidewalks waiting to die.

Hunger was not the only cause of death in the ghetto; diseases spread as well. Typhus, dysentery and tuberculosis could not be contained. But, of course, the Germans refused to allow medical supplies to enter the ghetto.

As hunger increased, so did smuggling. There were smugglers for profit–professional smugglers –and private smugglers. The professional smugglers did very well. The private smugglers were mostly women and children. Every day, they put themselves at risk by crossing to the Aryan side to sell meager belongings for a slice of bread or a few potatoes just to save their families from death. Many were captured and shot on the spot. There were two types of people in the ghetto: those who had everything—the newly rich professional smugglers, Jewish policemen, and officials—and those who were dying from starvation. If it hadn't been for the private smugglers, the ghetto would have never survived.

Actually, there were three classes of people in the ghetto. The smallest group, which numbered from 20,000 to 36,000, were the social elites, the professional smugglers, *Judenrat* employees, policemen, and other councils. The second group of people, numbering about 250,000, lived on the streets with no shoes or clothing, begging and dying. And then there were all the rest, who were still clean, still clothed, and who still had shoes on their feet.

The streets of the ghetto would be empty at seven o'clock in the evening, when curfew began. The Germans would march the alleys, their routine consisting of shooting people they found on the streets, or taking people out of their homes to shoot them for fun. They would leave the bodies on the sidewalks. Sometimes in the mornings, someone would cover them with old newspapers. They would sometimes lie for hours until the undertakers arrived. Nobody cared. Death became an everyday routine. **Not one day or night of peace occurred in the ghetto; it was simply one long nightmare.** No where were you able to find a tree, a flower, a bird or a butterfly; those were luxuries that didn't belong in the ghetto.

The Germans would come into the ghetto with clubs in their hands, and abuse Jews walking the narrow streets for no other reason than the fact that they could. They would walk from one side of the street to the other beating anyone in their way. Even before the Nazis began deporting massive numbers of Jews from the ghetto to Treblinka extermination camp, over 100,000 died from rampant disease and from starvation.

And yet, despite the grave hardships, life in the Warsaw Ghetto was rich with educational and cultural activities conducted by underground organizations. Hospitals, public soup kitchens, orphanages, refugee centers and recreational facilities all were formed in the ghetto. There was even a school system, and when a certain school was deemed illegal, it would still operate under the guise of being a soup kitchen.

There were even secret libraries, classes for children, theater, and a symphony orchestra. There was an underground network of religious schools for boys and girls, and institutions for advanced Jewish studies. These schools were a place of refuge for thousands of children and teens, as well as hundreds of teachers. In 1941, when the Germans officially allowed the local *Judenrat* to open schools, those schools already in place came out of hiding and began to receive financial support from the official Jewish community.

Several thousands of the people had worked in German factories that produced army uniforms, military equipment, and helmets. The pay for a 14-hour workday was either minimum wage or nothing at all, and the only hope the workers had was that they wouldn't be deported to the east. Thousands of Jews worked as forced labor outside the ghetto as well.

June 1941

On June 22, 1941, the Germans launched Operation Barbarossa, an all-out assault on the Soviet Union. Poland hoped for a Soviet victory, but that hope died as the German army quickly advanced across the Soviet Union. On June 24, the Germans entered Vilna, a city in Lithuania, which the Soviets had left in October 1939. When Napoleon passed through Vilna in 1812, he dubbed it "the Jerusalem of the north" because of the Jewish influence there (Napoleon may have been a visionary; in 1799 he invited Jews from Africa and Asia to join his army to "reestablish ancient Jerusalem"). By World War II, Vilna's Jewish population was 57,000, and on July 4, 1941, the Germans began to systematically kill Vilna's Jews. During just two separate actions that August, 10,000 Jews were taken to Ponary, a suburb of Vilna, and were shot 10 at a time. The victims were stripped before being massacred. In all, between 50,000 and 70,000 Jews were murdered at the Ponary woods. This was the first actual mass murder of Jews, and was conducted by the Germans in collaboration with the Lithuanians.

Vilna's underground organization was able to get messages into other Polish cities and to the Warsaw Ghetto: "Hitler is planning to exterminate the European Jewry," starting with the Jews of Vilna. Vilna also tried to convince Polish Jews that they should organize an armed resistance movement. By the end of 1941, other stories of methodical murder began to arrive in the ghetto as well. Messengers from Vilna risked their lives to get to Warsaw with many stories.

Most Warsaw Jews belonged to one of many political organizations. Some Jewish leaders had stayed behind, though most were able to escape to the Soviet Union. The messengers organized the meetings and explained what was going on in Vilna, that the Germans were killing all the Jews. The answer they received was that this could never happed in Warsaw. This was Warsaw, not Vilna. After all that had occurred, the leaders of Warsaw's Jewish community still didn't believe this sort of thing could happen.

At first, no one was thinking about organizing a resistence. Only a small number of people—from a different political organization—took heed to the warnings, and were convinced of the dangers. They decided to arm themselves.

Meanwhile, Berlin had already discussed the "Final Solution" on the subject of European Jews, and the decision to exterminate the Jews in the Warsaw Ghetto was approved. Beginning on July 22, 1942, deportations from the ghetto to Treblinka extermination camp began. In a two-month period, 250,000 Warsaw Jews and 100,000 Jews from other areas were sent to Treblinka. There, they were separated by sex, stripped of their clothing and other possessions, and marched to "bathhouses." It was there that they were gassed with Carbon Monoxide and, in later days, Zyklon-B. In numbers of Jews exterminated, Treblinka ranked only second to Auschwitz, with 700,000 killed at Treblinka and 1.1 to 1.5 million at Auschwitz.

The Germans let the chairman of the *Judenrat* know that, beginning that first day and every day thereafter, 6,000 Jews would be transferred out of the ghetto. And so, the Warsaw ghetto Jews awoke to a terrible new reality.

This is how the transfers occurred. A large force of Latvian, Lithuanian, and Ukrainian soldiers entered the ghetto, with more soldiers stationed on the other side of the ghetto walls. Platoons of armed Latvian soldiers wearing black uniforms and caps, marched toward the Umschlagplatz, a square near the railroad tracks. The square was surrounded with barbed wire and patrolled by armed police. This would be the assembly point for Jews who were taken off the streets.

In Umschlagplatz, before trasfer to Treblinka

All across the ghetto, posters announced the evacuation of all Jews, regardless of age or sex. They were allowed to take up to 15 kilos of luggage, plus all their jewelry. People arrived at the railroad tracks believing they were being sent to better conditions in labor camps to the east.

Loading the cattle cars. About 100 Jews were crowded into each car and then the door was shut and locked from the outside.

But the Germans weren't satisfied with the daily number, 6,000. They then demanded that 7,000 be shipped each day. Jews were picked up off the streets, taken from homes, beaten and whipped and dragged to the square. When the square was full they were loaded into cattle cars. Once the door of a cattle car was sealed, the only air that entered came from a small window that was covered by barbed wire.

The trains were made up of between 70 and 80 cattle cars, each holding 120 people. No one sat down, and families were separated. On the roofs of the cars, Ukrainian troops manned machine guns. Back in the square, those who remained waited for hours until the next train arrived. While they were waiting, soldiers shot at them, and when there weren't enough trains they simply waited for days without food or water. The Ukrainians would select young, pretty girls and savegly rape them, then kill them.

Soon, the daily quota rose from 7,000 to 10,000. By then, whole streets were being emptied, and it was impossible to avoid the Jewish police. They began to forcefully gather Jews in what was called an *Aktzia* (action), and by this time no one knew at all what their fate may be.

On July 23, the leader of the *Judenrat*, Adam Czrniakow, was ordered by the SS to deliver 7,000 Jews, followed by 10,000 every day after, to the railroad station. If Czrniakow knew what was about to happen, we'll never know: he committed suicide without leaving a note. Following his death, the Jewish police took complete control of delivering the victims to the Umschlagsplatz, a square in the ghetto surrounded with barbed wire, to be deported to the gas chambers at Treblinka.

The Germans promised bread to anyone who reported to the square, and out of desperate hunger many took them up on the offer. On July 31, the Germans took over the roundups of people. The cruelty is impossible to describe. People being shot in cold blood, elderly people being thrown out of windows to smash into the street, children stabbed with bayonets, babies swung against walls until they either quit crying or died.

Approximately 6,000 Jews were shot during the *Aktzia*. In 1942, between 254,000 and 300,000 Jews had been sent to Treblinka, where they were murdered. Cattles trains from Warsaw mostly went to a single location: Treblinka.

When there were just 55,000 Jews left in the Warsaw Ghetto, the decision was made to fight. Most who fought were young men and women. One of the leaders was Mordechai Anielewicz, from the Jewish Fighting Organization (ZOB), and the other, who historians omit, was Pawel Frenkel, from the Jewish Military Organization (ZZW). During the *Aktzia*, underground organizations told the people to hide and to disobey the German and Jewish Polish. They were repeatedly told that Treblinka was a death camp. Some of these underground leaders were caught, tortured, and shot.

As an incentive, the Germans promised three kilos of bread and one kilo of jam to those coming
to Umschlagplatz voluntarily

One of the first acts of the Jewish underground in the ghetto was to execute the commander of the Jewish police, a cruel Jew who had chosen to work hand-in-hand with the Germans. Others were given notice: if they were traitors to the Jewish people, their fate would be the same. There was a new rule in the ghetto: cooperate with the underground. When the issue of raising funds for weapons arose, the rich were made to give. One way or another.

Mordechai Anielewicz's dream was to go to Israel. He was selected to lead the uprising in the ghetto, but there was a small problem: during the *aktzia*, several of the young fighters and some of the leaders had been swept up and sent to Treblinka. The biggest shipment of weapons was gone, as it had been discovered by the Germans. They eventually were able to obtain some weapons from the Polish underground. They received a shipment of pistols, grenades, and explosives. The price of one pistol purchased from Polish profiteers had reached 10,000 zloty.

In the months prior to the uprising, members of the ZOB managed also to smuggle large numbers of arms into the ghetto by bribing German and Polish police. After that, nearly every member of the underground was equipped with a pistol, and several of them had grenades.

On January 9, 1943, Heinrich Himmler, who led the Gestapo and was second in command to Hitler, and was in charge of Hitler's "Final Solution" (the extermination of the Jews), visited the Warsaw Ghetto. He learned from reports that there were over 40,000 Jews in the ghetto working in German factories or in private Jewish shops. Himmler refused to listen to the SS Commander in Warsaw, Colonel Von Sammern, that Jewish forced labor was helping the German war effort, and ordered SS General Kreiger to expel the 8,000 Jews working in private shops immediately. This was to occur on Monday, January 19, 1943, the day known as "Surprise Monday."

The Germans hid their intentions well. Colonel Von Sammern deployed Latvian and Lithuanian collaborators for the operation. The German police and Wehrmacht soldiers that were destined to go off to fight the Soviet Red Army also participated. These soldiers were given a boost to their morale in preparation for future battles by being allowed to kill Jews in the ghetto first. This would give them their first taste of victory.

On January 19, 1943, after nearly four months without a deportation, the Germans blocked all the exits and suddenly entered the ghetto. They shot 600 and rounded up another 5,000 in a very short time. They first arrested hundreds of those who were used for forced labor. They were joined by passers-by before they could hide. Then the Germans went to the hosptial and took patients and medical staff. There, if you couldn't walk you were shot. Others were killed while they were being taken to the Umschlagplatz. The Germans only managed to collect 3,000 Jews, as some simply disobeyed shouted orders, hiding in places that had been prepared in advance. The Germans would surround a building, burst into apartments, and pull families out onto the streets.

At this point, the ZOB was not yet fully organized, and the weapons they had were still not distributed to all the Jewish fighters. Had the decision to fight come sooner, perhaps they would have succeeded this day. But at this point, the ZOB consisted in theory only. Beginning that day, January 19, the Germans were no longer total masters of the streets in the Warsaw Ghetto.

On the morning of January 18, most of the ZOB members had gathered on Mila Street. The next day the Germans arrived on Mila Street, shouting for everyone to get dressed and get out of their homes. The fighters were still not organized. Mordechai Anielewicz made a quick decision: they would hide their grenades and pistols and mix in with the Jews who were being deported. The Germans expected no resistance, and didn't know that the fighters had moved into position, and when Anielewicz gave the signal, for the very first time in the ghetto it was the Germans who cried for help as bullets and fragments of grenades ripped their flesh. In the end, only Anielewicz survived. The first Jewish armed resisitance began that day, and the fighters actually had some success. But mostly it was satisfaction, a payback. From that day on, fighting would take place from house to house.

The Jewish fighters had been preparing to resist since the previous fall, and the Germans didn't think that the Jews would continue to fight. They considered this an isolated incident, a one-time event. But now, for the first time, they were met with opposition. Armed Jews opened fire at them from stairwells. They fought from houses and on rooftops; they threw Germans from fourth and fifth floor windows; they chased after Germans armed only with a pistol and a "Molotov Cocktail." The Jews fought.

This *aktzia* only lasted four days, with only 6,500 Jews being rounded up for deportation. The deportations stopped, and the resistance took control of the ghetto. It created shelters and fought against collaborators. After several losses, the Germans were no longer allowed to go into attics, on top floors and down into cellars. They also started moving cautiously when they were on the streets. This January uprising became a prelude for the great uprising that began three months later on April 19, 1943.

The ZOB and the ZZW (under the command of Pawel Frenkel) took these months to plan their future resistance. They created hiding places, dug defensive bunkers and tunnels to plant mines beneath the streets the Germans would primarily use. Most importantly, the ZOB and the ZZW got as many weapons as they could. Jewish forced laborers who worked in German uniform plants smuggled pieces of German uniforms for the fighters.

On April 18, 1943, senior SS officers in Warsaw held a special meeting. SS Police General Juergen Stroop was there, a relatively unknown SS officer who had been appointed by Heinrich Himmler to command a special operation designed to liquidate the ghetto. In the operation—this final *aktzia*—the German force would consist of 36 officers, 2,054 soldiers brought in specifically for the operation, and 13,000 other soldiers. Adolf Hitler's birthday was on April 20, and this would be a special gift from Himmler to his Fuhrer. General Stroop saw no issues in being able to deliver that gift.

Outside the ghetto, resistance against the Germans and other collaborators was mostly impossible. But there were some places it was possible. Some success occurred in the Polish and Russian forests. Many Jews joined up with Russian partisans, and in some cases partisan groups consisted of only Jewish fighters. One such group were the Bielski brothers. They organized their own group of Jewish partisans. They saved over 1,200 Jews and ambushed German troops on their way to the Russian front. They blew up trains and other important German installations.

Inside the Warsaw ghetto the story was different. **This was the first place where an organized resistance against the undefeated Nazi-occupiers occurred.** The uprising went unnoticed in all other countries, and, besides certain individual people, the Polish population did not encourage or help the uprising. They didn't think that young Jews inside the ghetto would be willing to fight to the end or die with dignity as their forefathers had for centuries in the Land of Israel. The courage and daring of the uprising lifted the pride and boosted the moral of Jews who were in hiding outside the ghetto as well, those on the Aryan side of the ghetto walls.

April 18, 1943 was the night of the Passover Seder. The Germans liked to surprise the Jews on their holidays, and April 18 was no exception. **They had crushed well-armed nations, and had sent million of defeneless Jew to slaughter without resistance. They had created prisons that were inhuman and the lowest forms of degredation. They had forced the Jews to obey their orders. There was no country to protect the Jews, because the Jews had no country of their own at that time. But the spark of resistance did not die out, the determination and pride of the people lingered in the air.** April 19th proved this to be true.

At 6:00 am on April 19, 1943, the German procession entered the Warsaw Ghetto from various directions. There were columns of soldiers, tanks, cannons, and armored cars. They were, of course, armed to the teeth, marching confidently through the streets. And they were singing.

At the first reports of these troop movements, ZOB commanders checked their sections. Each fighter had a pistol, 15 bullets, five grenades, and five Molotov cocktails. The Germans did not expect much resistance, let alone an ambush, so when the Jewish fighters suddenly opened fire on them the Germans sustained heavy casulties, with many dead and wounded. They stopped marching in the streets, and split into smaller groups, moving under cover of fire from building to building. On that first day, the Germans only rounded up 580 Jews, though all were shot dead.

On April 20, 1943, Hitler's 54th birthday, Himmler had to postpone his birthday present. Not only were the Jews fighting, but they were inflicting casualties upon the Germans. Finally realizing that there was an armed combat force in the ghetto that they were certain would not easily give up, the Germans advanced into the ghetto, burning building after building. Some fighters managed to escape through tunnels they'd dug beneath the ghetto walls; others were not so lucky. One of the groups was turned over to the Germans by their Polish escorts. 631 bunkers and dug outs were discovered by the Germans during the uprising, which they, in turn, destroyed.

Some Poles were filled with pride when they heard that the Jews in the ghetto were fighting back and when they saw the two flags—Jewish and Polish—flying over Muranowska Street. They hadn't thought the Jews were capable of doing so. (Of course, they must not have remembered the Old Testament descriptions of the great Jewish armies of ancient times.) Jewish women fought side-by-side with their male counterparts in the up-

April 18, 1943:General Stroop arrives in the Warsaw Ghetto.

April 19, 1943:The beginning of the Great Operations, battles on Zamenhoff and Nalewki Streets. Two tanks are destroy4d. Van Sammern is relieved of command.

April 20, 1943:Fighting in the area of the brush plants and Toebbens-Schultz. The Israeli and Polish flags are raised in Muranow Square. The Polish underground attacks German positions. Hitler's 54th birthday is celebrated in Berlin.

April 21, 1943:5,200 Jews are evacuated from Toebbens-Schultz and transported to labor camps. Fighting in Muranow Square. The fighters in the brush plants area break into the central ghetto.

April 22, 1943:Stroop orders the ghetto to be set on fire.

April 22, 1943:The Germans wipe out a group of Beitar fighters who had managed to escape the ghetto and were hiding in Otobocek.

April 23, 1943:The organization moves its headquarter out of the bunker at 29 Mila Street. Anielewic in a letter to Antek Zuckerman: "My life's dream has come true." The Germans execute the Judenrat chairman, Marek Lichtenbojm and his deputies.

April 24, 1943:Thousands of Jews are expelled from the area of the brush plants. Himmler intervenes on behalf of Stroop in the disagreement between the latter and Glubotznick.

April 27, 1943:The Germans execute 120 Beitar fighters captured in a house in the Polish section.

April 29, 1943:40 fighters manage to get out of Toebbens-Schultz through the sewage system. Stroop orders Warsaw municipality engineers to blow up dams in the trenches in order to drown the people hiding there.

May 2, 1943:SS General Krueger arrives in Warsaw to observe the battles. Stroop arranges the execution for him of hundreds of Jews who had been captured in the Brauer plant during the Aktzia.

May 3, 1943:The Germans discover the bunker on 30 Franciszkanska Street. Many fighters are killed during two days of fighting.

May 7, 1943:The Germans comb the area of Mila 18 in an attempt to discover the headquarters bunker.

May 8, 1943:The headquarters bunker on Mila 18 is liquidated. Mordechai Anielewicz, 100 fighters, and about 200 civilians are killed. The survivor attempt to escape through the sewage system.

May 10, 1943:The survivors of the Mila 18 bunker and other fighters manage to get out of the sewage pipes on the Aryan side.

May 12, 1943:Stroop orders the small ghetto on Prosta Street to be set on fire.

May 16, 1943:Stroop informs his SS commanders: "The Warsaw Ghetto is free of Jews." The large synagogue on Tlomackie Street is set on fire.

June 18, 1943:Stroop is awarded the Iron Cross First Class, in recognition of his service in Warsaw.

rising, which amazed the Germans. This was an unexpected turn for them, female fighters.

While the Germans continued to burn their way into the ghetto, people attempting to escape the burning buildings were machine-gunned as they came out. There are many stories of great bravery, heroism, and suffering during the uprising. There was very little help from the outside, and yet, incredibly, it took the Germans more than a month—and much spilling of their blood—to defeat the ghetto fighters. It had gone from street to street, house to house, bunker to bunker. In the end, however, there were simply too few Jewish fighters left. Some escaped to join partisan units, and many fought to their last bullet, murdered later by the Germans or sent to concentration camps like Treblinka, Auschwitz-Berkenau, or to labor camps, where death was a daily occurrence. Some saved their last bullet for their own use. Many were pulled from their bunkers and shot on the spot, or gassed while they were still in the bunkers. Mordechai Anielewicz, the leader of the ZOB, was killed in one of the bunkers. He is still remembered in Israel, where there is a kibbutz named in his honor "Yad Mordechai." He was just 24 years old when he died.

The Underground Leaders

Mordechai Anielewicz: died in Mila 18 during the Great Uprising.
Mordechai Tenenbaum: died in the uprising against the German occupier in the Bialystok ghetto.
Joseph Kaplan: was killed by the Gestapo in September 1942.
Zivia Lubetkin: survived the uprising and immigrated to Israel.
Yitzhak Zuckerman: survived the uprising and immigrated to Israel.

Mordechai Tenenbaum

Mordechai Anielewicz

Joseph Kaplan

Yitzhak Zuckerman "Antek"

Zivia Lubetkin

The underground leaders of the left-wing party in the Warsaw Ghetto

Pawel Frenkel

There are many excellent books about Mordechai Anielewicz, the courageous leader of the Warsaw ghetto uprising. But there was another courageous leader in the uprising whose story was never told and who was treated unfairly, and whose name won't be found in the history books. The public's understanding of the uprising in the ghetto is only half of the story; the other half came to life much later. That story is of its unsung hero, Pawel Frenkel.

For many years, the mother of my friend Yehuda Hartman, Ziuta Rotenberg-Hartman, whom I knew, tried to tell the story of that forgotten courageous leader, Pawel Frenkel. There are those in Israel who didn't want to listen to her. In fact, David Ben-Gurion, who was on the left side politically, did not want it to be publicized. Politics played a big role in this. Anielewicz was from the socialist left-wing side, Hashomer Hatzair, which was the ZOB youth movement.

Just recently, Pawel Frankel's true story as an unsung hero from the gheto uprising came to light.

He was a 23-year-old activist, and was from the right-wing Betar group, the ZZW. Prior to the start of World War II, Frenkel underwent training by a local cell of the Irgun (one of the right-wing Zionist underground militias based in British-held Palestine and Ze'ev Jabotinsky and Menachem Begin's party). Frenkel was being prepared to fight against the Nazis. There is no known photograph of him other than a sketch drawn from memory.

The reason that the story of the uprising is generally a one-sided story stems from the ideological differences that split the Jews both before the war and after they were in the ghetto. Back then, youth movements were extremely political, and rivalries between the groups governed relationships, even in the ghetto. Had they been able to have united, perhaps more Jews would have survived. At any rate, when two member's from Anielewicz's ZOB organization told the story of the uprising after the war, they concentrated only on what the socialist, left-wing side had done. Frenkel and his group on the right were edited out of the story.

Pawel Frenkel was highly devoted to the cause of fighting the Germans and to sacrificing his own life to do so. His fighters carried out the extermination of the informers that existed in the Jewish police and in the *Judenrat*, those Jews who had spied on the behalf of the Gestapo. Frenkel's group was also responsible for posting the warnings in the ghetto, and for communicating the need for the people to fight. His group worked as a military unit and was divided into different departments: medical, legal, rescue, communications, finance, information, and military. Each department had a leader who was responsible for that section.

Frenkel and his fighters bore the brunt during clashes on Muranowska Square, and hoisted the Jewish and Polish flags over 17 Muranowska Street. The flags flew for four days before the Nazis finally shot them down. For years, no one mentioned those courageious fighter, and their stories did not appear in any history book. In 1966, Chaim Litai Lazar wrote the book, *Muranowsky 7 (The Warsaw Ghetto Rising)*. The book is based on evidence gathered from identified sources. In 2011, Moshe Arens book, "Flags over the Warsaw Ghetto," finally brought that great story to light. It is a great book. Some of the information comes directly from the diary of SS Police General Juergen Stroop, who received the Iron Cross First Class for the Warsaw Ghetto "Action." Stroop's own detailed 75-page report on the suppression of the uprising was later used as evidence in his trial. The title of the report was "The Jewish Quarter of Warsaw Is No More." Stroop was sent to Poland after the war, where he was executed. Another excellent book about the Warsaw Ghetto uprising is *Mila 18*, by Leon Uris (fiction).

A new movie made in Israel, "Remember Them All," is about the Warsaw Ghetto fighting. In Arizona, I'm the only one with the rights to the copy.

Pawel Frenkiel

Ziuta Hartman

Ziuta Rotenberg-Hartman, my friend's mother, took part in the uprising and fought alongside Pawel Frenkel. She passed through the Umschlagplatz, and was deported to Treblinka before being sent to a camp at Skarzysko Kamienna. In 1944, Ziuta was working in a weapons factory in Leipzig, where she was located at the time of the liberation just days before the official end of the war. After the war, Ziuta Hartman made a vow never to return to Poland as she crossed over the border into Czechoslovakia. She received an invitation to go to the Royal Castle in Warsaw, the official residence of Poland's past monarchs, to receive an honorary citizenship for her participation in the Warsaw ghetto uprising given to her by the city council. Maintaining her vow, Zuita refused to go. On July 31, 2010, in the presence of former Polish President Alexander Kwasniewski, her two sons went to the ceremony in Warsaw to accept the award for her. - B. Oct. 5, 1922, D. May 19, 2015.

By the way, in Treblinka a group of Jewish prisoners made plans for their own uprising. They had learned about the uprising in the Warsaw Ghetto, and this strengthened their morale and motivated them to revolt and plan a mass escape. They began their revolt on August 2, 1943. It is estimated that about 300 people escaped Treblinka, but only 100 of these survived the ensuing SS manhunt.

Jan Karski

In 1942, Jan Karski was preparing for another dangerous journey to England on behalf of the Polish underground. That summer the extermination of the Jewish population had reached a crecendo, and thousands of Warsaw Jews had been sent to the Treblinka extermination camp to be gassed and burned upon arrival.

Karski had been instructed by the Polish underground to meet with two Jewish leaders from the ghetto, who described the situation to him and asked for help from world leaders. Karski then asked them to smuggle him into the ghetto to see with his own eyes the mass roundups of Jews, which they did. Later, dressed in a Latvian guard uniform, Karski was smuggled inside one of the camps. There, he witnessed the brutality that accompanied the unloading of Jews from deportation trains, and took his eyewitness accounts with him when he traveled to London and Washington.

In London, Karski provided his reports to the Polish government-in-exile, and was scheduled to meet with Prime Minister Winston Churchill, who, however, was too occupied to see him. In the United States, Karski met with President Franklin Roosevelt, who listened attentively to his narration of what was occurring inside Poland. They spoke for almost an hour and a half. Later, when it came to the discussion of Jewish topics, Karski could feel that his report was falling on deaf ears. Roosevelt seemed to want to avoid the Jewish issue. Instead, Roosevelt asked Karski how the Germans were treating Polish horses.

In his book, Karski wrote: "All those great individuals, Presidents, Ambassadors, Cardinals, who said they were shocked: they lied. They knew or didn't want to know."

Had the allies acted on Karski's information, millions could have been saved. Perhaps the Poles could have saved more of their own countrymen, the Polish Jews. But Jewish blood is also on the hands of those who certainly were able to do something, yet did nothing.

Diplomats

During World War II, diplomats and people in other high positions and from different countries saved thousands of Jewish lives. Here are a few of their names:

Ciune Sugihara	Japanese diplomat
Feng-Shan Ho	Chinese diplomat
Georg Ferdinand Duckwitz	German member of the Nazi party
Frank Foley	British secret service agent
Giorgio Perlasca	Italian
Raoul Wallenberg	Swedish humanitarian
Colonel Arturo Castellanos	El Salvadorian diplomat
Abdol Hossein	Iranian diplomat
Aristdes De Sousa Mendes	Portugese diplomat
Dimitar Peshev	Deputy speaker of Bulgaria
Hiram Bingham	American diplomat
Selahattin Vikumen	Turkish diplomat
Gosques Saldivar	Mexican diplomat
Professor Aage Bartelsen	Leader of the Danish underground
Varian Fry	American journalist

This list is by no means all-inclusive, as there were many others who saved Jewish lives. I must add one other person to this list, however: Lyndon Baines Johnson.

In 1938 and 1939, Lyndon Johnson was a young congressman from Texas. He supplied visas to Warsaw Jews and oversaw the illegal immigration of hundreds of Jews through the port of Galveston, Texas. In 1960, Lyndon Johnson became Vice President, and from 1963-1969 was the 36th president of the United States.

Letters from Students and Faculty-Part 1

I have received many, many letters over the years from both children and adults who have attended my talks and wish to share their feelings with me, or thank me for sharing my story with them. I have selected some of them to print here. I have made no changes to these letters other than omitting the last names.

First, I want to highlight an essay sent to me from Coatimundi Middle School in Rio Rico, Arizona, after the students there found out my husband Gerry had fallen ill with incurable cancer. I received the essay along with the teacher's note:

Wanda,
I had told my enrichment class about your husband (the class you talked to) and one student made this for you.
Mary Kotnour

Mary's Class

I'm so sorry to hear abut your husband. My class and I give you both our best wishes. I would offer my sympathy, but I think you both are too strong to accept it, and I'm sorry if I'm wrong about that, though. I think that the best thing you can do is be happy about the times you've had and enjoy the times you're having. I know it's hard to lose a loved one, and that's what I'd do, but I've never been in your exact position so I'm not exactly sure what you're going through. No one really does. But you do have many people watching out for you two and supporting you both. You're not alone in this, neither of you are.

To wrap this letter up, I'm sorry for the longest, send my sincere apologies, hopes and wishes. I'm sure many do.

Shayla

Speaking to students

"Faith in Humanity" Essay
Excerpts from Coatimundi Middle School Student's Essay
Rio Rico, Arizona

To me faith in humanity means that in the darkest times and the rainiest days people will show some kind of sympathy to those in need, no matter what the personal gain is for that person who gave up, in the very least, their time and effort. Faith in humanity to me also means that nobody would ever kill somebody in cold blood. Faith in humanity is what keeps those in need alive and able to enjoy another day without fear that somebody may hurt or steal from them in any way.

Faith in humanity to me, is acceptance. Acceptance to everyone, race, religion, sexuality, and all other things that people can categorize someone in, without ever knowing who they really are. We were not placed on this earth to divide into groups and shine a light on each other's differences and flaws, as if anyone is perfect. No one is perfect, but everyone can have peace.

To me faith in humanity means you have faith that the community you live in will do the right thing under any situation. Also that you stand up for what you believe in and what you think is right. Being proud of where you live and the people you are surrounded by because you know they will do what's right for them and the community not because they are forced to but because they want to. Trying to understand something in someone else's point of view gives a chance to have faith in humanity.

To make a difference, we first need to make sure this never happens again. We can start by each one of us respecting everyone, no matter what they do or say. Because if we don't, the same war may start again all because of judgment of people who are different. Though that's what makes each one of us special and unique, our differences!"

"To put faith in humanity in action, you have to show your kindness and that you care. If I see someone being bullied, I could stand up for them or report it. If someone's making a racist joke, I could tell them to stop. If someone is being prejudice, I could tell them to stop. Just little acts of kindness and by helping people, even in small ways, a difference can be made. It can also give someone faith in humanity.

Some things I, and others can do to put faith in humanity into action is just the little things we do. It can be as simple as holding the door open for someone or asking if someone's okay if they fall. Some big ways can also be speaking up when you believe something is right or wrong. Maybe you can even stand up for someone if you see them being bullied instead of just standing there and being a bystander. Just by doing that and having the guts to do it, you could maybe even change the life of the person who's being bullied. You could give them the faith in humanity they need. Any act of kindness you do can help start putting faith in humanity into action.

~~~

Dear Wanda,

I just wanted to thank you so much for all the time and effort you put into promoting the Holocaust Exhibit in the gallery. That evening show .... when our only visitor was you .. oh my goodness .... what a visitor you were and turned out to be. From then on you were diligent... working to get the word out regarding this show.

Your story...told as a survivor of the Warsaw Ghetto ...touched the students as well as Jaline and myself. It became real, hearing how you survived such things at a very young age and how courageous your mother was to bring you both through this alive. Then leaving Poland to the new Israel, joining the military ... a woman ... what a story ... what a woman. Thank you again for all you have done.

Vicki

~~~

Dear Wanda,

I want to thank you from deep in my heart for coming and speaking with my students. They actually constructed the last quarter of the class. We watched the film, "Freedom Writers' which made them want to read Anne Frank and we went from there. Your talk was very inspiring. Part of our theme was truth. They were all speaking their truth and it was wonderful of you to come and share yours.

I also appreciated that your story helped them put their own stories in perspective. Not everyone was able to write a thank you because we were at the very end of our school year and some did not complete. But you got them there that day. That was most of my three classes in attendance. Of the ones who did write, _____'s father is a crack head and has never been part of his life. He wrote that his dad once stole his new shoes three days before school started to sell for drugs. His older brother is in jail. _____'s brother's gang involvements led him to stab a boy to death in Tucson. He is doing 25 years. His words do not reflect how deep his feelings go. He also has a brother doing time. _____ is another "fatherless" boy. He sees his dad in the neighborhood from time to time but they do not speak. _____ lost his father to an overdose when he was six. His brother was recently released from prison. And _____ is doing well. Her father abandoned them to alcohol a long time ago, but her mother has found a new husband who has been a father to her.

I hope you enjoy the photos and their letters.

Sincerely,

～～～

Hey Wanda,

I just wanted to drop you a quick note and say thanks again for coming and sharing with us.

The kids seemed to really enjoy it as did the adults. I had them write me ½ a page about what they thought and how it made them feel. Many of them said they felt like crying to hear what some people had done to others. Many also stated that it really got them thinking about how important it is to be nice to each other and to stick up for one another. A few stated that they had been making a conscious effort to be nicer to others.

I think you had quite a positive impact on several of them.

The best of wishes.

～～～

Wanda,

What a wonderful piece and picture about you, and I thank you for all of society. Your indomitable drive and dedication is an inspiration for us all - makes us work a little harder, stand a little straighter, and get to it. What a terrible it would be for humanity if you did not leave these memories of what we know to be facts for generations to come - know that you are appreciated.

Hope you are well. Fondly, Joan

～～～

Dear Wanda,

Thank you so much for giving your time and speaking at the Holocaust vigil. Your story was truly inspiring, and made us stop and think about our lives. It was a real honor to have you as a speaker. Feedback from the students were so positive and without you, the 16th Annual Holocaust Vigil wouldn't have been as successful as it was.

Thank you again! 24-Hour Holocaust Remembrance co-chairs,

~~~

Dear Mrs. Wolosky,

Thank you for teaching us about your life. Your presentation was a very nice thing to learn about a wonderful lesson.

You taught me many things. I didn't know that Jesus Christ was Jewish. Also, I didn't know that you hid with Catholic family. I cannot imagine what it would be like to have no food or water for 6 day.

You also taught me that life is short to not throw it away. The gave me courage to tell my friend to stop thinking of killing herself.

Also you thought me to respect people that have different races. Now I think it is more important than never to stick up other people. For example on day in softball game one of my friends was scared of ants. One ants climbed up her legs. She started to yell. All of the girls laughed. I said how would you feel if people were laughing at you I also remember when people used to call me names because I have a birth mark in my face. It made feel sad and anger. I hope I don't ever make someone feel that way.

Thank you again for coming to speak to our class. I hope that I will never let anyone be bullied. I will always remember that.

Sincerely,

~~~

Dear Wanda,

With a full spirit and an ever thanking heart, we thank you for giving us the privilege of meeting you and being able to hear your story. We express our sincerest sorrow and sympathy with the many things you had to deal with as such a small child. If at all possible we would return to you the childhood that was stripped away from you. You are truly an inspiration to all of us. Your strength give us strength and you story helps us better understand what was happening during that dreadful time. Even though your start to life was burdened with pain and sorrow, you have lived a fulfilling life. You are an example to all of us. Thank you for being who you are and sharing your history with us.

~~~

Dear Mrs. Wolosky:

Thank you for telling us about life time and what happened to you. Your presentation was great and I learned a lot.

I didn't know that Christ was Jewish. I also didn't know that you went to the army. I want to go to the army too.

You also taught me that you should stick up for others and your self. Also, life is short and too precious to throw it away so I'm keeping it.

It has changed me to start treating every body equally. It has also changed me to not call people mean words because it can come back to hurt you and it hurts others.

Thank you again for coming to speak to our class about your life. I hope that you can come visit us again.

Sincerely,

~ ~ ~

Dear Mrs. Wolosky,

Thank you for coming here and telling us about your experience. Your presentation was the best.

First, you have taught us how life can be so important. For example. you thought us to enjoy every moment of our life. Now that I know that, I now plan to spent more time with my family. Also, you taught us that how can life be so important because it is Ilk a gift, but a really big gift. Another thing you taught us is to appreciate what we have in life. I mean there is some people that just because they don't like how a food looks they sometimes just through it away. There is other people that have to eat a little bit of rice.

Finally, I just want to say that you taught us lots of things, but important things. So thank you for your time and sharing your experience to us.

Sincerely,

~ ~ ~

Mrs. Wolosky

I think you're a great, courageous and brave woman! I really do admire you lots. Hope God gives you many many more years life. I learned to value life more thanks to you, if you were able to get through that horrible situation, then I am sure I can be strong too. Take care. Thanks for letting me write about you.

~ ~ ~

Dear Mrs. Wanda Wolosky

I wanted to thank you for coming to Middle school to talk about your life and what you went through during the Holocaust. / honestly don't think I would have lasted a week without food or water My grandfather use to be a prisoner of war during World War II. He would tell me the most horrible stories I could ever imagine. He would tell me how the Nazi's would kill children, while the mother's watched, and how they would smash babies into the ground. I don't know which concentration camp he was at, but it sounded like a really horrible one. My grandfather was eventually rescued after escaping with 3 others and was given a medal called the "Medal of Honor" for being a World War hero.

Sincerely,

~ ~ ~

Dear Mrs. Wolosky,

Thank you for coming to our school to tell us about your life during the holocaust, how you survived, and generally what was going on in Poland at that time. I know that it must be really painful to bring up those memories about what happened to your friends and family. It must be hard growing up with a religion that you truly believe in, but it also one of the mos discriminated against religions in the history of the world, Judaism. Many groups have tried to destroy Judaism, the Crusaders, the KKK, the Pogroms when people killed Jews, and then the Nazis who killed more than six million Jews and other "impure" people. I hope that you will keep coming to this school to tell people like me about the terrible things that occurred, so that they will know and that they will remember that this did happen no matter what other people may thing or say. Thank you, your story made me think about the holocaust much more seriously.

Sincerely,

~ ~ ~

Mrs. Wanda -

I want to express to you my gratitude. You are a woman of great strenght and courage. Thank you for sharing your story. You have helped me see a different light.

Forever in my prayers -

God Bless

~ ~ ~

Dear Mrs. Wolosky,

Your story really opened my heart, and made me realize the pain all of those Jews went through. You did nothing to deserve that kind of torture. It is very hard concept to grasp at my age, but I would like you to know how grateful I am you took time out of your life to tell my classmates and I your story.

My mother passed away a few weeks ago, and I have been thinking that its the worst thing that could happen, and that no one else could ever feel as much pain as me. Your story of being so mistreated because your religious beliefs throughout your life has really showed me that I should be very grateful of what I have instead of sobbing about what is gone. I had no idea that so many innocent people had their lives taken away and terribly traumatized because of Hitler's selfish reasoning. You are so strong to have kept your head up during such a terrible time. It is people like you that keep the world spinning round!

Thank you very much for giving me a new, strong perspective of life. I will always remember you and your story. And we will all pass it on to our children and grandchildren to make sure nothing like this could ever happen to another soul. I hope you have a wonderful year, and many more.

Sincerely,

~ ~ ~

Dear Mrs. Wolosky

Danke/Thank you for sharing your story it was sad and enlightening. / never knew how much trouble and pain you must have gone through. My great grandfather was in WWII but I just thought that the Germans were attacking us not committing a mass genocide of the Jewish community. Your story was truly moving. Next time someone is talking about WWII I will share your story.

I will always remember your story in my heart. / hope you will share your story for years to come. Danke for the most moving story l have ever know. It was great for you to come and share it.

Sincerely,

~ ~ ~

Dear Mrs. Wolosky,

Hi my name is Mohammad. I am II years old and in sixth grade. I enjoyed learning about the Holocaust from a person who witnessed it from her own eyes. I was touched by what you said, it made me and I think a lot of other people sad to listen to what you had to say. So thank you for teaching us something we could have never learned from a textbook or just from taking notes. I was glad to learn all these new things from you.

There is one thing you told us that I will remember for the rest of my life and that is when you were lucky enough to escape from the Nazis and get safely to Israel. Also I have learned to always have hope no matter what happens to you or your family. I learned this from you because you were lucky enough to make all the way to Israel. Than you ounce again for coming to our school to teach us.

Sincerely,

~ ~

Dear Mrs. Wolosky

Thank you for coming in and telling us your story. I know it was hard for you because it was like living it all over again. Also I'm very sorry for your losses, but I'm glad you survived. You also inspired me because you never gave up even though times were tough. Also you inspired to stand up to myself, and to help someone when they're in need. Your story really spoke to me because I didn't really know much about the holocaust before you told your story and I thank you for that.

I will always remember your story and how it affected me. I will always remember those poor people who died, and what the German soldiers did to the people in those times. When I think of the holocaust I think of my uncle because he died in the holocaust at the age of 17. I wish I could've met him, but I met you. You gave me a story that I will share with my kids and their kids etc... because that's how much it touched me. I will always remember the day that you spoke to the class. I will always remember how brave you were when you told us your story and I thank you for that.

Sincerely,

~ ~

Dear Mrs. Wolosky.

Thank you so much for coming down and telling us about your heartfelt stories. This is a big deal that we got to hear your stories as many other schools don't get this opportunity. Your stories were very detailed and easy to understand and listen too, you have great speaking skills. My grandmother was born in 1933 and she lived in Italy for a few years, she could not give me stories as detailed as yours were. You had funny stories such as the rabbit stem and very sad they both touched my heart deeply, and I will always remember this experience.

Sincerely

~ ~ ~

Dear Mrs. Wolosky,

I wanted to thank you so much for coming and sharing your story with the class. It was very interesting to hear your story. Never in a million years would I be able to be as brave as you. I can't believe what you went through. It must have been very hard for you. You had a lot of strength and a brave heart.

If was sad to hear your story because it seemed like you went through so much pain and tears. I am truly sorry that you went through that hard experience. I pretty much cried during your story. I can't even believe that happened. It was very cruel and very unfair. bid you ever feel like you wanted to give up? While listening to your story if was very scary for me.

You are truly my #1 hero!! I look up to you and I want to be just like you! Brave and Kind! I am so thankful that I got to listen to your story; I'm sorry for what happened.

Thank you for being brave!

Love:

~ ~ ~

Dear Mrs. Wolosky,

Thank you so much for coming to tell us your story. You must have been very brave to live through the Holocaust. You story was a story like no other, a story of bravery, inner strength, sorrow, and survival. I am very grateful that there are still survivors from that horrible time. I was very moved by your story and that you came and shared it with us, that must have been very hard for you to relive that horrific history. Your story really touched my heart and made me look at life in a whole different way. Life is like a flower, if you lost a petal you can grow it back, it you don't get water you will die, if you get too much water you will be wilted, and if you are taken care you will thrive. I liked when you added the story about the cat. It was admirable and funny, When you add some small light funny stories in your story I think people would enjoy it more and they would learn to be happy for the survivors of a sad time.

Sincerely,

~ ~ ~

Dear Mrs. Wolosky,

Thank you for coming to our school and telling us your story. Your strength was truly amazing, it was just as inspiring as your story. I was impressed at how strong you were even in the face of huge injustice. I was also truly amazed at how you were able to talk about all the horrible things that happened to you and still stay calm and composed. It must have been much harder then it looked as when I reported on one of the holocaust survivors I had troubles staying composed. I admire this.

I plan to take your story and remember how you and many others suffered due to discrimination and how easy it is to prevent it. I hope this will keep me from discriminating against others. I believe discrimination is a huge problem and needs to be kept in check as in history it has caused numerous deaths and much other grief. If this can be stopped or at least be minimized by talking about the problems it has caused I think that the stories need to be spread. Thank you for sharing your story with our school.

Sincerely,

~ ~ ~

Dear Mrs. Wolosky,

Your story was filled with devastation, joy, and terror and I am so pleased that I was able to hear you talk about your experience during World War Two. I never realized how severe the persecution was against Jews, through the brief history you gave I learned about the unfair lifestyle that you, and many before you, had in Poland. To go through the worst imaginable circumstances as a young girl seems to have made you a very strong woman. I was able to visualize the brutal conditions of the ghetto and imagine the fear you must have felt.

Hearing of the dead bodies in the street made me realize just how awful the German soldiers could be. It is crazy that people could do something so evil but remarkable that you were able to live through it. Escaping the ghetto must have taken a great sum of courage from you and your mother. It was so sad to discover that many of your relatives were not as fortunate as you.

I loved listening to you tell all of your different stories. It was really interesting to learn about your life in hiding after escaping the ghetto. I also valued all that you had to say about Israel. To go to a new place where freedom was all that was needed seemed like the most joyous thing. Thank you for sharing your difficult childhood memories and uplifting life with us so that we are able to understand the cruelty that was inflicted upon you and millions of others.

Sincerely,

~ ~ ~

Dear Mrs. Wolosky,

Thank you so much for coming and speaking to us. Your story was amazing, and it taught me to stand up for what I believe in. It's not every day when people who survived the Holocaust get to speak to kids like me, so thank you for give me an opportunity to listen !!

~ ~ ~

Dear Mrs. Wolosky,

I'd like to say thank you for coming out and telling us your personal story about your experiences in the holocaust. I think that your story put a huge impact on how I am as a person and it gave me a new perspective on life. I think what shocked me the most was how young you were when all this was happening and the sacrifices you went through just to survive. When you were telling the story about your mother gave the bread that was meant for your family to that lady that was your neighbor even after she was being rude and inconsiderate really made me think that after that day she helped you guys out and gave you a place to live just because of what your mother did really made me think that if I'm nice to everyone, even if their not to me good things can happen. That story really made me change from how I used to be, I used to just think for myself and nobody else and after you left I respect my family and friends and I tell them something nice every day before I leave because one day they might not be there. Once again I'd really like to say thank you for coming in and sharing your experiences with us, because of your story I have become a better person.

~ ~ ~

Dear Mrs. Wolosky,

I would like you to know how grateful I am for you coming to our class. / am so glad we had the privilege to hear such a touching, firsthand experience. / remember when our teacher first mentioned that you might be coming: / got very excited because / had always wanted to hear what it was like instead of just reading it from a book. When she announced that you would be sharing your stony with us I was immediately looking forward to it. World War II and the holocaust are my favorite times in history, because / think we can learn the most from these events.

It wasn't until you finished your stony that / realized how hard living in that time must have been for such a young girl. I am amazed that you were able to present to us such a detailed stony, and I greatly appreciate it. Your stony showed me just how brave the people who went through the war had to be. I don't think I would be able to have the kind of strength that you had to get through it all.

For me, this experience really helped me understand what kind of things happened at that time. I find myself incredibly lucky to have gotten to hear you speak, and / thank you for sharing your time with us.

Sincerely,

~~~

Dear Mrs. Wolosky,

I would like to thank you for coming into my class. It was a really great experience for me. The Holocaust is my favorite time in history to study. I found your talk extremely inspirational. You are such a brave and strong person. I am not sure that many other people could have gone through that.

I once read the following quote, "those who cannot remember the past are condemned to repeat it". It is so important for children to learn and understand the past. We would never want the Holocaust to happen again. That's why having survivors like you speak to our classes is so important. We all can learn from your stories. Thank you once again.

Sincerely,

~~~

Dear Mrs. Wolosky,

Thank you so much for coming to speak. It was truly a once in a lifetime experience to hear you. I really admire what you do because I know it must be very difficult to recount such painful memories so often. It is very important that we never forget the Holocaust, lest something like it happen again.

You are an incredibly brave and strong person to have survived that ordeal, and to choose to tell your story to children afterwards. Being Jewish myself, I felt I had a deeper connection to the things you were saying, more so than some of the other students. After hearing you, I feel extremely lucky to have been born where I was when I was. Because of the courage of people like you and my grandparents, I am able to live a comfortable life here.

We read in textbooks about these things, but when you spoke, it truly made it come alive. Speaking for my other classmates, we are all very thankful and appreciative, myself included. It broadened and expanded our knowledge of World War II on a personal level, which is an opportunity most people never get to have.

It was an honor to hear you and an experience I will never forget. Thank you again.
Sincerely,

~~~

Dear Mrs. Wolosky,
I am pleased you decided to share your experiences; it was a very extraordinary experience. Your presentation was very touching. It is important to know about the sometimes forgotten times of the holocaust. As time goes by history fades in the minds of the public. As the inevitable darkness falls over the events of the holocaust your story will illuminate these times and allow the next generation to see the often agonizing and shameful truth. If history does repeat itself, you telling your story will prevent it. Your presentation has shown me the darkest deaths of human behavior. The deepest levels of evil are many time rooted in prejudice. Your presentation has not only informed me but shown me that I cannot let the world of the future repeat its mistakes. We appreciate your story though many times it is hard to talk about such things, you have told us your story and we appreciate it.
Sincerely,

~~~

Dear Mrs. Wolosky,
First of all I would like to thank you for visiting my school and sharing your experience during the holocaust. We know that it was not easy talking about the subject and it took a lot of courage and strength to talk about it once more. We all greatly appreciate your effort and I have learned a lot about how life was during those times and how difficult

it was to survive each and every day. You are truly a symbol of great heart and a sense of determination to all, showing you striving to keep alive and well during all those years of hiding and secrecy.

You have taught me a countless amount of things that I take for granted until this day. You have taught us all our freedoms that we are given to us when we are born such as our right of speech. We are able to say anything we want freely about almost anything, anywhere we want. The right to own land, and living without the fear that you have to be under constant watch, and being fearful of being spotted and being killed because of your race or religion. We have to be more thankful of everything we have and everything that is given to us. That is something that I will never try to ever take for granted again.

Having you talk to us has enlightened me, and has taught me so many things about the war that I didn't know before. When you had explained to us about you lived in the ghetto, and the almost unsustainable living habits that they had you placed under, made me see that we should be thankful and more understanding of the holocaust and the horrible circumstances that you were placed under. You have helped not just me, but I'm sure many other students understanding what difficulties you have surpassed.

Thank you again Mrs. Wolosky for your presentation of your life during the holocaust. It was very interesting and I have learned a lot. I have very much enjoyed your presentation and would love to hear from you again.

Sincerely,

～～～

Dear Mrs. Wolosky,

We would like to thank you for coming to visit our class to talk about your childhood in the Warsaw Ghetto. You story was ultimately inspiring. The events you described gave us a better understanding of how horrible life was like for the Jews Ic the Warsaw Ghetto during World War 2. We realized, through you story, that many of the things we need for simple survival today were denied for the millions of Jews who suffered under the Nazis brutality. Many of the events in your story were shocking, such as when you described how the Nazis tormented he Jews. The most shocking detail, in our opinion, was when you described how a Nazis would pick up a Jewish child by their feet and knock his head against the wall. The Nazis were unbelievably cruel to the Jews.

The moment we found most memorable was when your mother gave the second loaf of bread to the women that didn't like you. This simple act became an important factor to your survival. Your story will be kept as a reminder of all the innocent Jews :hat died in the Holocaust and the many more who never stopped fighting for their lives. We will also tell your story to other, hoping that they find your story and your strength as inspiring as we do. Whenever we see someone being persecuted for heir race, religion, gender, etc. we will not just stand by and watch, we will do something to stop it. Thank you once again for your time.

~ ~ ~

Dear Ms. Wolosky,

I would like to thank you for coming and speaking to our class. It cannot be easy to recall and retell memories of such times, and I truly appreciate your coming and doing it. I thought your life story was remarkable, and I was, without a doubt, affected by it. There is a definite difference between reading about something like the Holocaust, and hearing it firsthand from someone who lived it.

I was amazed by your courage. Living through such a thing, I I thought it was incredible that you and your mother were so strong-willed. I think the entire class was surprised by how discriminated against Jews were, especially with the explanation of the rough times you had experienced as a preschooler. I admire that you were so courageous even at such a young age, standing up for the small girl that had waited in line for the swings.

I thought it was incredibly selfless of your mother to give that loaf of bread to the woman, even though you had others to feed. I think that is an incredible show of courage as well. Your story really made the entire class sit down and listen quietly, with real interest. It's not often that one is able to do that.

The fact that your story was told from a child's point of view made it easier for us to identify with it. It made me stop and think, "what would I do in a situation like yours?" It made me imagine living in such times and hardships, and I know that it would be incredibly hard. That makes you even more admirable. It is evident that you are strong, and were strong even as a child. As children, we rely others, and everyone around us. You and your mother relied on each other.

I find you to be a figure to look up to. Your life is something that I will always be able to look back on. I will always remember the story of a girl, who, though all odds were against her, was able to fight through and stay alive. I think everyone who was listening to your story would agree when I say, you are someone amazing, and someone I can look up to. Once again, thank you for coming to our class, and telling us your life story from a personal experience.

Sincerely,

~ ~ ~

Dear Mrs. Wolosky:

It was such an honor to listen to you talk on Friday. I /earned so much more in those two hours about the Holocaust then I will ever learn from a book. Your story is such an inspiring one, one that I will take with me for the rest of my life. I cannot even begin to imagine all the things you went through. You provided us with an experience that most children do not get to go through. In twenty years, there will not be anymore survivors, so this experience will be a once in a life time thing. I have honestly never thought of how much we take advantage of our freedom here in the United States, until you told your story You gave us great advice, to stand us for what is right, because we can here in America. I just hope that when Jam your age, lain as strong and forgiving as you are. Thank you so much again for coming to tell us your story.

Respectfully and thankfully,

~ ~ ~

Dear Mrs. Wolosky,

Thank you so much for coming to talk to my class about your experiences during the Holocaust and WWII. My name is Carly and I'm and 8th grader. I truly appreciated your speech and the complete honesty you had about what occurred. I really learned so much in the hour and a half that you spoke to us. My understanding of the Holocaust is so much greater from listening to you.

From reading my textbook, The Diary of Anne Frank and Night I learned about concentration camps, life in hiding and factual events of the Holocaust. However, I didn't really understand what life was like for the people of the time. From your talk I did experience this greatly along with the emotions of the time. From your speech I also realized the great bravery of thousands of people, such as your mother. But, I was most moved by the strength of a people, even under dire circumstances, In fact, the part of your speech that stuck with the most was when you said how you sneaked out to look at the burning ghetto, and how you began to cry because you wanted to be there to help fight against such a great evil. I believe that one quote from your speech will stay in my mind for a very longtime, because of the potent and raw emotion of your love of justice.

I really appreciate you telling your story. I can only imagine how hard it must be to re-live those memories several times a day. You have forever changed my understanding of WWII and your story will stay with me for years to come. Thank you so very much

for sharing with my classmates and myself.
Sincerely,

~~~

Dear Mrs. Wolosky,

The opportunity that you gave my classmates and I was great! When heard you were coming I was so eager to talk to you. couldn't believe I was going to have a chance to learn about the Holocaust from a primary source. What you did was very smart and heroic. I learned so much from the presentation and your story, it was much easier to understand than how the books explain it. Your advice was great The one that I really related to was when you told us not to be afraid of the bully. When get bullied or my friends get bullied I always protect them and myself. I am really thankful for having you over and now I'll be able to inform people about the Holocaust and how I got to talk to a survivor.

Thank you for spending your time with us and sharing your story. This was a very interesting story. You went through so much and still led a great life. I don't know how I can thank you for coming over, it was such a great experience to have you over. All your experiences that you shared with us made me understand the Holocaust so much better. I'll say it again Thank You so much for coming to Desert Shadows Middle School and speaking to us.
Sincerely,

~~~

Dear Mrs. Wanda Wolosky,

Thank you so much for coming to our middle school to share your life story during the Holocaust. I can hardly imagine how horrible it must have been living in a ghetto. I admire you for being so strong while keeping your faith and hope during a horrible time in history.

Your story helped me appreciate what I have. For example, you mentioned how you had very little food and water, and you went days without eating or drinking. I realized how lucky and how happy I should be that I have access to food and water. Even those distasteful green vegetables I can't stand.

Again, thank you so much for coming to our middle school to discuss your life story You really changed how I see the world I live in and helped me appreciate the little things I have.
Sincerely,

~ ~ ~

Dear Mrs. Wolosky,

Thank you for coming to tell us you very touching story. I can't believe what you went through at such a young age. I was very touch with your story because with every thing you went through proves you are tough and strong. When you said you promised never to cry in public meant the most to me because I have tried to make that promise before. But I didn't make it. You are a very strong independent woman. You are the person I will look up to from now on. I started tearing up while you were talking because I kept trying to put myself in your shoes and be were you are today. I wouldn't have made it. You are my new role model.

Sincerely,

~ ~ ~

Letters from Mansfield Middle School:

You made me feel like my life isn't hard even though I'm poor and I live in the ghetto and my Dad is in rehab for heroin you made me think life can be harder so thank you M. Wolosky you really changed my life...

We have to remember what we did in the past, so we never do it again, and we can use it as a reference point for the future...

Your story is so inspiring and I loved listening to you tell it. And I figure if you can get through all of that and not kill yourself during, I can win over suicide too...

When you explained how you stood up to that bully at school, it touched my heart. From now on I'll be as brave as you were during the holocaust. Than you for that very important lesson...

I thought your story was amazing how you told it. I think everyone who heard it would agree. Since we're the new generation of people, we will carry this story on. Especially to my children and grandchildren...

You made me think of life in a different way. We need to not take it for granted and be thankful for what we got...

~~~

Letters from other Middle School Students:

When you were telling the story about your mother gave the bread that was meant for your family to the lady that was your neighbor even after she was being rude...really made me think that that day she helped you guys out and gave you a place to live just because of what your other did really made me think that if I'm nice to everyone, even if they're not to me, good things can happen. I have become a better person...

Ever since I was little I have been intrigued by world war two and Holocaust. I have just always thought "you know that's not how it really happened. It wasn't that bad." But now I see that it <u>was</u> how it really happened, it was really that bad, that horrible...

I have honestly never thought of how much we take advantage of our freedom here in the United States, until you told us your story. You gave us great advice, to stand up for what is right, because we can here in America...

~~~

From Orange Grove Middle School

We need to know what happened during the Holocaust. We need to be aware that not everyone has freedom, and the liberties that we have today could vanish if another evil person such as Adolf Hitler takes over control with false promises of a better world...

~~~

From Baboquivari Middle School

I also want to thank you for teaching me to stand up for my people and nation. You have inspired me to keep working towards my goal of attending Harvard University and giving my nation recognition...

~ ~ ~

From Coati Mundi Middle School

You also taught me that life is short and to not throw it away. This gives me courage to tell my friend to stop thinking of killing herself...

~ ~ ~

From Altar Valley Middle School

I thought it was good of you to forgive everyone who hurt you. I liked that you said nobody can live with hatred for the rest of your life. That's a good reason to forgive someone...

~ ~ ~

Dear Wanda,
Your visit to Castle Dome Middle School, Yuma, Arizona, meant a lot to students and staff. It meant a lot to me to be able to meet you at the house in Yuma. My first husband was Jewish and I always enjoyed his family, his synagogue as well as the timelessness of the Jewish religion.
Sincerely,
Harriet E. Williams, Principal

~ ~ ~

Dear Mrs. Wanda Wolosky,
I am an 8th grade student at S.M.S. and I would like to thank you for coming to my school and telling us your life story.
I am very thankful that you were kind enough to share your story. It opened up my eyes to see how bad it really was. I saw movies and read books on it but it was different hearing it from you. I really understand how bad it was.
Thank you again for taking your time to come speak to us.
Sincerely,

~ ~ ~

Dear Mrs. Wanda Wolosky,

I am writing this letter to tell you how much your story has inspired me. As you shared your brave story I imagined myself in your shoes throughout the whole time. I asked myself how would I do this or for that matter how were you able to stay out of harms way so many times.

You not only escaped with your freedom you escaped with your life, and for what you had ended as a child during that time I find you truly brave. I thank you very much for coming to our school and sharing your tragic tale and for also inspiring me in the way that you did.

Sincerely,

~ ~ ~

Dear Mrs. Wolosky,

I hadn't perceived all of those feelings you displayed during your presentation by taking notes through Ms. Ambroziak, but now I have a better understanding of not only the events in the Holocaust but the emotions during the process.

I think that it really is amazing that you survived, considering the treacherous circumstances facing you, such as the smuggling and the hiding.

I am very glad you decided to start going around to classrooms and sharing your experience with us. I agree that it is very important for preteens and teenagers like ourselves to hear these accounts of Hitler's cruelty to Jews and other 'undesirables' firsthand. Your story is amazing, and I am glad that you came to our particular classroom. Ms. Ambroziak has spoke fondly of you in the days leading up to your visit.

Your visit to our classroom was a life changing experience for me. It was hard to believe that Hitler could do all of those terrible things, but while you were talking the experience really came alive for me, and I am thankful for that. I hope you continue this and keep going to classes and telling your story.

Thanks,

~ ~ ~

Dear Mrs. Wolosky,

Everyone found it extremely inspirational and it was an honor to have you there. You helped me to see what that that era was like from the first-hand perspective, and learn more about the atrocities of the Holocaust then textbooks and biographies combined had taught.

It was really touching that you were able to stay strong through all of the things that you went through; it shows that you are a brave person, and I will forever look up to you for that. Speaking of the lady that you gave bread to, and how it changed her, was what touched me most, because it showed that kindness will continually be spread even in the darkest of times. You endured so much more in your youth and were tested more than I, and it's made you into a better person than many of the people that I know, including myself. Being able to stand up in front of a classroom, and educate them about such hard experiences must not be an easy task, but it is a task that will help the youth of today to put aside our differences and assure another holocaust will not be in the future.

I wish you luck in whatever you do next. Your speech has made me a better person, and I hope that future speeches will continue to help children like myself to also become better individuals.

Sincerely,

~ ~ ~

Dear Mrs. Wolosky,

Danke/thank you for sharing your story it was sad and enlightening. I never knew how much trouble and pain you must've gone through. My great-grandfather was in World War II but I just thought that the Germans were attacking us not committing mass genocide of the Jewish community. Your story was truly moving. Next time someone is talking about WWII I will share your story.

I will always remember your story in my heart. I hope you will share your story for years to come. Danke for the most moving story I have ever known. It was great for you to come and share it.

Sincerely,

~ ~ ~

Dear Mrs. Wolosky,

I know it was hard for you because it was like living it all over again. Also I'm very sorry for your losses, but I'm glad you survived. You also inspired me because you never gave up even though times were tough. Also you inspired to stand up to myself, and to help someone when they're in need. Your story really spoke to me because I didn't really know much about the Holocaust before you told your story and I thank you for that.

I will always remember your story and how it affected me. I will always remember those poor people who died, and what the German soldiers did to the people in those times. When I think of the Holocaust I think of my uncle because he died in the Holocaust at the age of 17. I wish I could've met him, but I met you. You gave me a story that I will share with my kids and their kids etc...because that's how much it touched me. I will always remember the day that you spoke to the class. I will always remember how brave you were when you told us your story and I thank you for that.

Sincerely,

~ ~ ~

Dear Mrs. Wolosky,

Hi, my name is Mohammad, I am 11 years old and in the sixth grade. I enjoyed learning about the Holocaust from the person who witnessed it from her own eyes. I was touched by what you said, it made me and I think a lot of other people sad to listen to what you had to say. So thank you for teaching us something we could have never learn from a textbook or from just taking notes. I was glad to learn all these new things from you.

There is one thing you told us that I will remember for the rest of my life and that is when you were lucky enough to escape from the Nazis and get safely to Israel. Also I have learned to always have hope no matter what happens to you or your family. I learned this from you because you were lucky enough to make all the way to Israel. Thank you once again for coming to our school to teach us.

Sincerely, Mohammad

~ ~ ~

Dear Mrs. Wolosky

My name is Antonia and I was one of the students who was listening to your incredible story. From what I have heard about the Holocaust, I know that it was a horrible time and lip for you to come and talk to us about everything that you went through is very brave, I know that I could have never done it.

When you were telling us about all of those rough times you had to go through with your mother I have to admit that I started tearing up and so did my friends. This happened because if I had ever gone through those horrible times, especially with my mother, I probably wouldn't have survived. If you've parts of the story made me laugh or chuckle a bit like when you told us about the cat being thrown out the window, but he still survived and that's why you believe cats have nine lives.

Also another part that was funny was when you told us about the big bunny that used to bite your toes. In conclusion I just wanted to let you know that your story taught me to never give up on what you believe is right and to always believe in yourself because there is always a good side to things. Thank you.

Sincerely,

~ ~ ~

Dear Mrs. Wolosky,

I just want to thank you for coming to our school and telling us your story. I told my sisters about your story and they said that they had heard her story before, when they went to my school. They asked me if I knew the story about the cat and I said, "yes."

My dad has a cousin who is a Holocaust survivor. Her name is Gloria and she lives in San Francisco. Gloria used to visit schools but now she's too old. She lives in a nursing home. She has a pretty cool story about how she survived the Holocaust. I know the story well enough to give you a picture in your head. It is kind of short because I don't know the whole story. When she was nine years old she was taken to a concentration camp. She was there for three years. Then one day they took a whole bunch of people to a forest where they were going to get executed. The guard said to her, "we are taking you to a place where you are going to get killed, if you want to live jump now, but if you get caught don't tell them that I let you live, because if you do I won't be able to help save other people." So then she jumped. For the next three days she hid under the snow. Then she saw a truck and the truck driver saw her. The truck driver pulled over and gave her a blanket. Then she got into the car and he took her to a place where she could be safe. She is in a book called The Jews in America.

I want to thank you again for coming. I learned a lot. When you were telling the bad parts it made me feel really bad. I even cried a little bit.

Sincerely,

~ ~ ~

Dear Mrs. Wolosky,

Thank you for coming to our school and sharing your experience with us. Your story was incredible and moving. I really got to learn a lot and also see how lucky I am to be living in a safe place.

When I visited my grandma in Poland she told me a lot about her experience and we got to visit the old ghetto of Poland. It was hard to hear how terrible and unfair people were treated. There were tears literally streaming down my face. I really appreciate your coming to our school and teaching us to stand up for ourselves and others about World War II.

Sincerely,

~~~

Dear Mrs. Wolosky,

Thank you for telling your story about the Holocaust. I have never heard a story like yours and in fact, I didn't know anything about the Holocaust until you told the story. You were and are very brave and strong about everything that was going on in that period of time. If I were there in your position during the Holocaust, I wouldn't have been as near as strong as you. When you told us about when you could hear the shooting in your sleep, I could hardly breathe. It was breathtaking. There have been a few times where I have experienced being horrified but your story is much more intense.

All of the details that you mentioned to us were shocking. I learned many life lessons from you. I learned what is right to do in a bad situation and to help others in need of help. Being safe it is important, you taught us much more about how to be safe. I have been thinking about the Holocaust and I realized that I don't think much about others and that I think about myself a lot. Now I know that it is very important to care for others too. I appreciate you coming to my school and telling your story.

Sincerely,

~~~

Dear Mrs. Wolosky,

Thank you for coming to our school to tell your story about the Holocaust to us. I really appreciate you giving us this experience because it is a really important story coming from a primary source. That is a really interesting story that touched my heart. I shared the story with all my family after school. I will spread that story through my family and they will spread it too.

Sincerely,

~~~

Dear Mrs. Wolosky,

I am writing from my school, and I'm a sixth grade student here. My name is Olivia. I am so thankful you came, and told you're amazing, and breathtaking stories! I was so excited to hear that you were coming to visit my class! We had learned a little bit about the Holocaust before you came, and I was so interested in learning more. I'm so happy you came. You really showed me how lucky I am to be able to live in such a great country such as the United States of America. Your stories were just incredible. Dig down in my heart I was hurting for you, I wanted to cry, but in the lesson you told me to be strong, to fight for what you believe in, and don't ever give up!

In that little bit of time you had with us, you taught me some amazing life lessons, which really touched my heart, along with others. It was truly amazing how your stories touched everyone in different ways, but they were also terrifying at the same time. I think you may have even become my new idol! You're so strong to have survived everything that you did. I feel very blessed to have been able to have you as a guest. I will make sure to share your stories with everyone I possibly can! I hope to pass on what you shared with me. I just want to let you know that it takes a very strong person to have survived the time period of the Holocaust. I was very moved and hope to learn more. I love your stories so very much, and hope to see you soon.

Sincerely,

~~~

From Hermosa Middle School

Presentation from a Holocaust survivor

The couple of weeks ago the sixth seventh and eighth graders got the privilege to get a presentation from a Holocaust survivor named Wanda Wolosky. She told us about her life in the Warsaw ghetto and events that happened, not just her personal experiences. We were honored to have her come and tell us about her personal experiences, especially since it is such a rare opportunity to have now. The students were very excited to have her come and we were intrigued by her story and experiences. It was a once in a lifetime experience for the students and we are so grateful to her for coming.

~ ~ ~

Dear Mrs. Wolosky,

First, I would like to say thank you for coming in and talking to us. Second, I want to thank you for sharing your stories with us. And third, I want to thank you for changing my life. You are a strong and brave person. You deserve to have a great life full of happiness. I'm sorry that you had a childhood full of hate.

I understand what it must've been like. Being scared, on edge, stressed, and worried. I know I can't compare but I have the same feelings so often. Some of the things you talked about, like not being treated fairly and being misused, I can relate. It is so hard for me to talk about it, I can't even imagine how hard it must have been for you. I wish I could go back and change what happened so you could have a happy child. Thank you and I'm sorry.

~ ~ ~

Dear Mrs. Wolosky,

Thank you for sharing your story. It was beautiful. In some ways I feel like I can relate to you. I too have been through dramatic experiences probably not as big as yours though. Again, I'd like to thank you. I'll always remember your story.

~ ~ ~

Dear Mrs. Wolosky,

Today your story greatly impacted me. Since I was 12 I've had a depression and anxiety disorder. I'll have random breakdowns and people always make fun of me and asked me what is wrong but the truth is that not even I know at times. Through the past years I've had no good relationship with either of my parents which very occasionally takes a toll on my heart. I've tried seeing love and care in the darkest of places and I come out of them more hurt than before. Your story inspired me today to keep going in the dark places. After hearing you speak and moving from there to seeing the title of your book, I was astonished. Your story inspired me that though my life may not be what I hope for, it's all I have. It is now my choice to step up and make it beautiful. Thank you. You give me hope.

Sincerely,

~~~

Dear Mrs. Wolosky,

It was such a blessing to have you come and talk to us. When you started talking about how you promised yourself that you would not let them see you cry and that you would be strong it really spoke to me because I remember having a similar moment when my dad left my mom, my five brothers and I. Our stories are very different but I want to thank you for showing me that you can get through tough struggles.

Sincerely,

~~~

Thank you for coming in and sharing your life during the Holocaust.

Thank you so much! We really appreciate you coming and telling us your story!

Your story was so interesting! Thank you so much for coming in.

Thank you so much for sharing your inspiring story with us!

Thank you so much for telling us your story! It really meant a lot to us!

To Wanda,

Todah Rabah from the entire seventh and eighth grade class for your inspiring and enlightening presentation. Your story is worth carrying on and sharing!

~~~

Dear Mrs. Wolosky,

Thank you so much for taking your time to come in and talk to us about the Holocaust; you were such a great inspiration. Your stories were so touching and helped me realize what was happening during the Holocaust. Your stories were very descriptive and help me create an image in my mind.

Your mottos that you go by really made me realize no matter what age you are if you believe in yourself and stay strong you can reach any goals you set for yourself. Knowing how young you were and what a terrible time you are going through but you still push through made me realize that no matter what the circumstances are you can find a way to manage. I really like how all your stories head lessons to be learned from them.

Your story about how your mother had to go up to the Nazi soldier, who would shoot anyone near him, and you had to ask him if you should go today or tomorrow really showed how much courage and bravery you have. This taught that to get past lots of things you need lots of courage and bravery which you have a ton of courage and bravery. I am so grateful that you came to teach us about the Holocaust; it was a great experience for me to have. Thank you so much for taking the time to come. I really appreciate it.

Sincerely,

~~~

Dear Mrs. Wanda Wolosky,

You were an amazing speaker for our class! I want to thank you for telling us what you had went through during those times of unspeakable horror. The way you talked about it had changed the way I look at the Holocaust and how I look at life. You made me realize that I am more than lucky to have to peaceful, free life that I am blessed with. From now on I will remind myself of what amazing things and privileges I have instead of complaining about the things I want. On top of that, the things I want are in no way meaningless and a distraction. You are the reason I am beginning to notice these things. Thank you for what you said to my class.

Sincerely,

~~~

Dear Mrs. Wolosky,

I would just like for you to know that your life story is a moving piece of history. Children of my age need to hear the stories from women like you who have seen terrible, awful things to keep the memory of what you have accomplished and went through so that we can try our best that something is awful as the Holocaust never happens again.

We also need to be able to know what happened during the Holocaust. We need to be aware that not everyone has freedom, and the liberties that we have today could vanish if another evil person such as Adolf Hitler takes over control with false promises of a better world.

I would also like to thank you for informing us what happened. Everyone in that room knew something about the Holocaust, but it's not as informative as a living person telling us the horrors that you and your generation went through. Thank you for taking time out of your day to tell us about your life story. Thank you for all of these things Mrs. Wolosky.

Sincerely,

~ ~ ~

Dear Mrs. Wolosky,

Thank you for coming in and telling us your experience about the Holocaust. I honestly really enjoyed it. And I think no one else can explain it better than you. The way you explained it really got to me like I was there at the Holocaust. You had so much detail and it got to me. I'm looking forward to reading your awesome book. I hope you come back in and hang out with us.

Sincerely,

Hope will come

Why can't darkness see the light
Why can't evil end up kind
With every word and every step
The world will grow like a sprouting plant
We all are equal though black and white
So why can't America see the light

By: Shelby

The Family 2013

Sharon and Chance

Lin and Paul

Jade

Jesse

This plaque was presented to the German Liaison Officers stationed at Fort Huachuca from the Holocaust Survivors in recognition of the friendship that was established between those two groups from 2003 to this day. The friendship became stronger with time. Each Officer, Sergeant Major and their families serve here for three years before returning to Germany. While they're assigned here, I invite them to gatherings at my home, and they invite me into their homes as well. We remain in close contact through email after they return to Germany.

Visiting Grand Canyon

First they came for the Socialists, and I DID NOT SPEAK OUT — Because I was not a Socialist. Then they came for the Trade Unionists, and I DID NOT SPEAK OUT — Because I was not a Trade Unionist. Then they came for the Jews, and I DID NOT SPEAK OUT — Because I was not a Jew. Then they came for me and THERE WAS NO ONE LEFT TO SPEAK FOR ME.

Pastor Martin Niemöller's poem

PHOTOS BY MELISSA MARSHALL • PHOTOS@SVHERALD.COM

Holocaust survivor Wanda Wolosky, lights one of the nine memorial candles during the Wednesday National Days of Remembrance event held on Fort Huachuca. Looking on is her grandson, Army Pvt. Chance Richwine.

From the Sierra Vista Herald newspaper, April, 2014. Grandson Chance and I lighting a candle during the National Days of Remembrance in Fort Huachuca

163

PLEASE JOIN US FOR THE

73RD ANNUAL MILITARY POLICE BALL

September 26, 2014

THUNDER MOUNTAIN ACTIVITY CENTER

BUILDING 70525

FORT HUACHUCA, AZ 85613

SOCIAL HOUR **5:00 PM**

RECEIVING LINE WILL COMMENCE AT **5:45 PM**

$30 PER MEAL

ONLY PERSONAL AND CASHIER CHECKS ACCEPTED

PLEASE MAKE ALL CHECKS PAYABLE TO **MPRA-THUNDER MOUNTAIN CHAPTER**

PLEASE ENCLOSE PAYMENT WITH RSVP

RSVP TO SSG DERRICK BRADFORD BY 08.31.2014

Sequence of Events

1700 Social Hour

1759 Call to Mess

1800 Welcome
Posting of the Colors
National Anthem

1835 Invocation (CHP Maglio)

1840 Toasts (See Program)

1845 Fallen Comrade Table Description

1850 MP Narrative

1900 Cake Cutting Ceremony

1905 Dinner Served

1945 Intermission

2000 Guest Speaker (Ms. Wanda Wolosky)

2035 Slide Show

2045 Closing Remarks (CPT Sproul)

2055 Benediction

2100 Retire the Colors

2105 Raffles

2110 Entertainment/Dancing – TMAC

2200 Conclusion

The Army Song

March along, sing our song, with the Army of the free.
Count the brave, count the true, who have fought to victory.
We're the Army and proud of our name!
We're the Army and proudly proclaim:

First to fight for the right, and to build The Nation's might,
And the Army Goes Rolling Along
Proud of all we have done,
Fighting till the battle's won,
And the Army Goes Rolling Along

Then it's hi! hi! hey!
The Army's on its way
Count off the cadence loud and strong
For where'er we go,
You will always know
That the Army Goes Rolling Along

MP Regimental March

We are the Regiment,
That of the troops was born.
We are the Regiment,
That for the troops was formed.
Military Police Corps
In peace and war is there
To assist, protect, defend our own
No matter when or where.

Lieutenant Colonel Milton Kelly was the Commander of Defense Logistics Agency, Distribution, Red River Army Depot, Texas. He was promoted and is now Colonel Kelly.

Some of the mementos from visiting different bases

Military Police K-9 Unit at Fort Huachuca, Arizona (US Army)

Being in a K-9 unit and interested in dogs, I found a very interesting story about a dog by the name of Stubby. It began during War World I. This was the time when one day Stubby wandered into camp of the 26 th infantry(Yankee), Division of Massachu-setts, and befriended the soldiers. In October 1917 when the unit shipped out to France, Stubby went with the unit, becoming "unofficial - official" mascot. Stubby did his part by providing morale-lifting visits up and down the line and occasional early warning about gas attacks or by waking a sleeping sentry to alert him to a German attack. One time Stubby got a little over enthusiastic and found himself on top of a trench when a German grenade went off wounding him. After his recovery, he received a blanket embroidered with the flags of the allies. The blanket also held his wound stripe, three service chevrons and the numerous medals, the first of which was presented to him in Neufchateau, the home of Joan of Arc.

He discovered a German Spy in hiding and was holding him pinned until the sol-diers arrived and captured him. Stubby confiscated the Germans' Iron Cross and wore it on the rear portion of his blanket. Stubby was also gassed a few times and eventually ended up in a hospital when his master, Corporal J. Robert Conroy, lay wounded. He remained with the unit till the end of the war and returned to the US. Oddly enough, this is not the end of the story. He was made a lifetime member of the American Legion and marched in every legion parade. He was so famous that the Grand Majestic Hotel in New York lifted its ban on dogs so Stubby could stay there. He met three US presidents: Wilson, Harding and Coolidge and was a lifetime member of the Red Cross and YMCA. Stubby served in seventeen battles. He receive a gold hero dog's medal, pinned on him by General Blackjack Pershing in 1921. In 1926 he passed on. He was the first and most decorated military dog.

Wanda

Letters – Part 2

In this chapter most of the letters are from friends and relatives–only some from recently visited places

Dear Wanda,

I'm sorry it has taken me this long to get these letters to you. When you read them, you will see how much you impacted and changed my students to whom you spoke. They will never forget you, and neither will I. it is beautiful to see the love you have in your heart for all people after what you have been through. I pray that your nightmares leave you. You really touched many of my kids who have also gone through very horrible things, and they found such strength and optimism for their own lives in your story. You are doing a very good thing for this world. I hope I can arrange for a much larger group to hear your story for next year...the more the better!

Sincerely,

Judy Ethington, Apollo Middle School eighth grade

~ ~ ~

Dear Wanda,

I just tried to call you but your line was busy. Anyway, I hope you are having as serene a Yom ha-Shoah as possible under the circumstances. I am still shocked and saddened to have learned of Gerry's passing, and want to wish you the greatest possible comfort during this hard time. I know you are strong—I read your whole books last night, and discussed it with my 10-year-old son—but please do not hesitate to ask me for anything if I can be of the slightest help.

Your book is everything you hoped it would be. The content and style are absolutely perfect for your intended audience (children, teens, very young adults). The narrative is very clear and direct, like you, and full of humanity and humor without being condescending to children. There is absolutely no schmaltz, and no nonsense, only hard crucial facts viewed from the point of view of someone who is, as one of the kids put it in her letter to you, "kind and brave." That is indeed what you are, in abundance. So was Gerry, and I am very honored to have met him. Zichrono libracha!!!

I am very proud that you have included my name in your list of acknowledgments. Thank you! I look forward to seeing you soon. Again, do not hesitate to call me if you want or need anything.

Best, David

~ ~ ~

Hi Wanda,

I finished reading your book, "After All: Life Can Be Beautiful." Thank you for sharing it with me and our students. It tells your story with such clarity, though it helps to have heard you in person, too. I've been to the Washington DC Holocaust Museum three times, and Yad Vashem twice. I come away speechless, so it makes me marvel even more at your journey and struggle to put something beyond words into words.

I hope you are adjusting to your husband's recent death, and finding a community of support. Even though you rightly wonder if God has been on a long vacation :), I offer my prayers that God dwells with you and your loved ones, and that God is providing your inner spirit was solace and love.

Shalom,

Ron Rude, Lutheran Campus Ministry, University of Arizona

~ ~ ~

Dear Wanda

You are an amazing woman! I am astonished and proud at how you have used your personal experiences and suffering from those terrible times, to educate audiences, especially German military audiences!

Think back in 1945, after you barely survived the Nazis and their death camps. Imagine that someone told you back then, that you would be living in Arizona years later and would become a speaker about your experiences to US audiences, including military organizations. Even more amazing, imagine that someone told you that you would travel to military bases where German Air Force and German Army units would host you, and want you to speak to them about your experiences. What an amazing turnaround in European history.

Cousin

~~~

Wanda—I love this speech! You inspire me every day to do better. Thank you for that gift.
R,
Kirby Olson
DLA Distribution Red River, EEO Office

~~~

Dearest Wanda,

Enclosed are the short notes that my social studies classes wrote to you. They have talked about you so much and they feel so privileged and blessed that they saw and heard someone who was in the war and suffered due to their culture and religion. It's hard to understand that concept without hearing someone talk about it and letting them know that it was true.

Thanks again for everything; especially for being a true and sincere friend. I look forward to seeing you soon. I will have to find a way of getting those books from you. I'll be in touch.

Sincerely and affectionately,
Rick Zamorano

~~~

Good morning Wanda,

Kay and I woke up thinking about your story this morning. We were very deeply touched. We knew your story would be hard to listen to and we did shed a few tears but we were not as depressed about it as I expected to be. I'm not sure why, really. Maybe because you survived after all and we could focus on that instead of the millions who did not. In the past, when we would read about the Holocaust, we didn't know any survivors in the focus just stayed on the millions upon millions who died and that is very depressing especially because in our hearts we have always known what the professor from NAU said yesterday—there are no "monsters" out there, that hatred can live in all of our hearts. And that is just so profoundly disturbing and depressing, and even hopeless. But then when a survivor speaks there is at least that ray of hope that some few, even a child, could be so strong as to survive and to tell the story—which must be very hard to do. And after all, we do need some little bit of hope.

I went 12 years to the second smallest school in Wisconsin. I learned of the Holocaust in our tiny library. Even though I was in high school at the time, I knew nothing about it. I was turning the pages of a big green book of wartime pictures from 1944 that had been published by Life magazine. I saw a lock of pictures in the front of the book of dead soldiers and bombed out cities. All this I knew about. But then suddenly I turned the page and there with the pictures, all of the famous ones, of the liberation of the concentration camps. The ovens, the piles of bodies, the gas chambers made to look like shower rooms, the medical "experiment," all of it. There was no one sitting next to me and I felt like standing up and saying out loud, "look at this! Did you know this!" But I sat quietly and kept turning the pages and I never mentioned them to anyone. As I looked at the pictures, I began to feel hollow inside. I was learning that the world was nothing like I thought it was. Maybe for the first time since seeing those pictures, I see a ray of hope or two after hearing your story.

(Kay here) I saw the trials at Nuremberg on Playhouse 90 (television) when I was in high school. I, too, saw the horrifying pictures from the camps as part of the trial evidence. Those images are everlasting. Having been lucky enough to be born in America, I can't imagine what it would've been like. Hearing your story makes it more real and personal. Thank you so much for sharing with us and the many people you have spoken to in the past.

Love,

Lloyd and Kay PS: I thought about telling you this last night, but I knew I couldn't get through it without bawling like a baby.

~ ~ ~

Wanda,

Speaking of amazing, I read your book soon after you gave it to me. I love it Wanda. It sounds just like you telling the story. It made me cry and it even made me chuckle— mostly of course, it made me cry. But your tough personality comes through as a child, a young woman, and later as an adult. your successes after the war makes it such an inspiring story as so many of the kids say in their letters to you. Kay and I are extremely proud of you and we feel privileged to know you. And Gerry too—I guess Kay mentioned that we stopped out to visit him. We each put a pebble on his temporary marker and on the Holocaust Memorial.

Love you,

Lloyd and Kay

~ ~ ~

A Word about Wanda Wolosky.

I met Wanda a number of years ago while she was a member of the Holocaust Survivors Group of Southern Arizona and I was the Facilitator of the group. One phrase to describe Wanda is that she is a force of nature. What that means to me is that Wanda is full of life, full of curiosity, full of discernment, and full of grit. Wanda tackles problems systematically and with gusto. In writing her book, Wanda would get up in the morning, go for her daily swim, write for a number of hours, and then go about the rest of her full day. Her full days include her love of opera, Broadway plays that come to Tucson's Centennial Hall, plays at The Arizona Theater Company and Gaslight Theater, and museum visits. She reads voraciously, and I don't believe I've seen her without a book in hand. She also checks in with her friends near and far, from her daughter and family in Sierra Vista, AZ, 'to her friends in Germany, Israel, and across the U.S. Then there are her hobbies: making little dolls, decorative lapel pins, and her fabulous cooking. She throws wonderful parties and get-togethers complete with her Jewish, Israeli, and Polish specialties. One never leaves her home without a to go box of a favorite dish. As she has been in Arizona, she has become enamored of Native American culture. She has annual trips to Pow-wows, gives talks to students in schools on the Reservation. Then there are her activities as a speaker on her experiences during the Holocaust in the Warsaw Ghetto. These talks include her numerous invitations to middle- and High Schools, to Universities, and to U. S. military bases across the country. Wanda also loves to travel and she has traveled extensively in her life. Her schedule is exhausting! And yet Wanda thrives with all this activity.

Wanda is a unique personality! I will say that she is deeply loyal to her friends and that when she gives you her word, you can depend upon it. She stands up for what she believes. I had lunch recently with Gail Wallen, Ph.D. who has been leading the effort to have Holocaust Survivors speak at military bases. Gail told me the story of a trip to Goodfellow Air Force Base in San Angelo, Texas. Gail had been listening to the weather report and there was an alert for a tornado near the base. Gail went to everyone's room and told them to go into the closet as the safest place to be in a tornado. When Gail got to Wanda's room, Wanda replied, "I've lived through worse" and went back to bed. That is Wanda in a nutshell. More recently Wanda was involved in a car accident not far from her home. Another motorist had not stopped and t-boned Wanda's car. Very calmly, Wanda called me from the emergency room at the then University Hospital Trauma Center.

She had the wherewithal to call her attorney, her insurance companies, and to cancel or postpone her theater tickets. Although she needed surgery and extensive treatment, Wanda was ready to think about sushi and barbeque instead of eating hospital food.

Personally, Wanda has taught me to be forward thinking, to be engaged socially, and to be an active member of my community. It is a great honor to hear of Wanda's life story. She inspires so many and she has inspired me.

Barbra Quade, LAMFT

Marriage and Family Therapist

Former Facilitator of the tlolocaust Survivors Group of Southern Arizona

~ ~ ~

Hello Wanda,

I started your book this afternoon and I could not put it down until I finished it. I expected it to be an emotional story, but I cannot tell you how many times I had tears in my eyes. I know you as a strong woman; now, I understand where that strength comes from. Your story story is a story of unbelievable resilience and I am proud to call you my friend.

Many times, when reflecting on my humble beginnings in the US, Think of you and how you helped me without asking anything in return. On many occasions I wondered why you were so good to me (and I know you have done this for many others like myself)—you took me in your house, Fed me, helped me find work, and were there for me anytime I needed a friend. I still remember the day you and Gerry took me to the bus station and gave me a $20 bill—that way I was able to travel to New York and live with that crazy woman.

Now, it all makes sense. You know what it means not to have much (not that my story compares to yours by any means) and to have someone who is willing to help you when you need it the most. Thank you again for being there for me.

Thank you for sharing your story and for making this world a bit better.

With humble admiration,

Cristina

~ ~ ~

Very touching letter!

Cristina put in writing my thoughts, it is exactly what I have always thought of you and Gerry...wonderful people... wonderful Jews... I always thought (before I met you) Jews were selfish, I was taught (in religion classes in school) not to help Jews, not to feed them and not to give them water... never to make a Jew my friend and I couldn't understand how come a Jew takes me to her house, feeds me, find me a job, even wants to ADOPT me...???

I was blessed to have met you and Gerry, may he rest in peace, you fed me, you have helped me (to this day) Como you made my dream come true, you encouraged me when I was weak and guided me towards the right path. You were the only people I had in this country, in this New World, you ARE my inspiration, OUR inspiration! Every time I go through the rough period in life, every time life challenges me (us) I think of you (of what you have been through) and that makes me stronger. Listening to you gives me strength and hope, gives me power to go on.

You are the reason I am here, in this country now, without you and Gerry I could have not done it, you are my second set of parents—I will never forget how happy Gerry was every time you guys pick me up in Tucson Airport at 4 AM shouting out my name with a big smile on his face "LILLYYYY!!!" With his arms up, wide-open... tears are rolling down my face every time I think of this...

I am so blessed to have met you, you are wonderful people, I will never be able to THANK YOU enough for what you have done for me and my family, the least I can do is go around and tell people that there are wonderful people out there... and they are "Jews."

I love you!

Lili

(Christina and Lili were working with me in the summer camp.)

~~~

Wanda is a wonderful woman who lives in Green Valley, Arizona. She is one of the millions of people that suffered in the Holocaust. She has and still does show courage in different ways. Courage doesn't mean you don't get afraid. Courage means you don't let fear stop you. Wanda, to this day, is a fearless hero who showed (and shows) courage. To begin with, she faced multiple challenges in her life. Most importantly, she was a Jew in the Holocaust. The Holocaust was an extremely tragic time in history when a man named Adolf Hitler and the Nazi party (the German army who followed Hitler's rule) Took more than 6 million innocent Jews (and 5 million others) from their family and homes into "concentration camps" where they were gassed in gas chambers, where put in working camps, where they die of hard work, hunger, thirst, weakness, and torture that is even too much to think about. Unfortunately, her father was killed by the Nazis.

Wonder faced extremely tough challenges and obstacles in her life. To pursue this further, she showed courage by taking risks. She smuggled food that was hitting on her body. This was definitely an act of courage because if the German soldiers were to find her, they would shoot her on the spot! According to After All: Life Can Be Beautiful, by Wanda Wolosky, it says: "the smugglers were mostly children and women. They put themselves at risk every day crossing to the Aryan Side to sell some meager belongings for a loaf of bread or a few potatoes to save their families from death. Many were captured by the guards and shot on the spot." As you can see, you can tell how risky that was. Lastly, after the liberation she emigrated to Israel and served in the Israeli army. And of course, being in the military is risky. Wanda showed courage in multiple ways, helping and inspiring others. Today, she speaks at military bases and schools to share her moving life story. She inspires soldiers, students, and teachers by giving speeches and helps others to this very day. She helped my mother when she needed it. For example, when my mom first immigrated from Romania to America, she had nothing but a few clothes. Wanda let her into her home, when she had no place to live, gave her a place to sleep, gave her food. And helped her find a job.

Annamaria and Lili

In the final analysis, Wanda is a hero. She puts others before herself, displays courage in many forms, and inspires people to try, take risks, and help. I know Wanda personally and she is like a grandmother to me. She promised never to cry again and still is standing strong to her word. She shows courage and support to many people.

Annamaria Ifrim, 11 years old

~~~

Something so hard it cannot be repeated.
Something so painful it cannot be ignored.

The pain that was felt by
fathers and mothers the pain
Of children who would never grow up

Why did it happen? Why did it occur?
What did any of them do to deserve?
Why did it happen and will again?
Can we stop it from happening again?
Can we try to fix mistakes?
Can we learn to show character traits?

Why do I see two eyes of hate
Staring at me to my face.
Am I different for some reason?
Is it my dark hair color for my facial traits
It my faith?
I'm God's child is it because of my
Heritage

2017, Kayalynn Eloria 10 years old
from Sierra Vista

Guest at the German Military Change of Command

Change of Command ceremony of the German Armed Forces Command
USA and Canada in Washington, D.C., November 2017

World War II Memorial in
Washington, D.C.

On behalf of the

Commander German Armed Forces Office

Rear Admiral Thomas J. Ernst

Defense Attaché of the Federal Republic of Germany in Washington D.C.

requests the pleasure of your company

Change of Command Ceremony
German Armed Forces Command
United States and Canada

Colonel (GS) Joachim W. Bohn

will relinquish command to

Colonel (GS) Helmut C. Frietzsche

Reception to follow

Please, join us
on Wednesday
November 22nd 2017
at twelve o'clock

at the GAFCOM International Airport Dulles Facility
23745 Autopilot Drive, Dulles, VA 20166

Dress Code:
Working Uniform
Business Attire

RSVP by Thursday, November 16, 2017
to: hanneloremeyer@bundeswehr.org

To expedite your entrance onto the GAFCOM Dulles Facility, please display this invitation and provide valid photo identification to the guard at the gate.
Your name will be verified and you may then proceed directly to the ceremony.

Invitation is non-transferable

December 13, 2017

Dear Ms. Wolosky,

On behalf of the entire JCMS 8th grade, we would like to thank you very much for coming to our school and sharing your personal experiences in the Warsaw Ghetto with us. your stories are truly heart breaking, and helped us realize how horrible the Holocaust was.

We just finished reading Elie Wiesel's book Night in our English classes. The book was painful to read, and it is hard to believe that this could ever happen. After listening to you speak, it all became very real. It means so much more to us to hear the story from a survivor standing before us all than reading it in a book.

We're so sorry that you had to go through such a horrible childhood. You are a very strong woman to have endured so much and survived all of the terrible things you had to go through.

Is is an honor to meet you, and we are very grateful to learn about the Holocaust from you. Thank you for taking your time to come and meet with us today.

Respectfully,
Melina Christopher, Kayleigh Mitchell, Samantha Beasley

March 16, 2018 – Sells

Wanda Wolosky years ago experienced scenes of tragedy and horror she can never forget and does not want to forget. For six years beginning in 1939 she and her mother survived day-to-day in the ghetto of Warsaw, Poland after the country was invaded by Nazi Germany in World War II. Wolosky told her story to students, faculty and community members at Tohono O'odham Community College's Main Campus on March 6.

She stayed silent about her Warsaw Ghetto experience for decades, but eventually she decided it was time to talk. She wrote about her life as a 5-year-old girl in Warsaw in a memoir, After All: Life Can Be Beautiful.

As Wolosky spoke to those gathered at TOCC, she looked at no notes, she spoke from memories that seemed etched into her mind. The details about which she spoke made a few listeners squirm in their chairs.

Without going into the sometimes uncomfortable story she told, suffice it say that what she saw when she was five, no child should see. "Life in the ghetto had little value if you were Jewish." Rotting bodies in the streets were a common sight, people were routinely stopped by Germans and stripped naked to be searched, homes were confiscated if not burned, and Wolosky drove home the point that hunger was a constant state. Her story is in the details. Lice were everywhere, even on the money used to buy what meager food was available. Families would scramble to get two potatoes so they could survive for one more day. Wolosky one day wrapped pig meat around her body under her clothes to sneak it home.

In the ghetto, she said, you got used to stepping between dead people–that was just life and death in the ghetto.

If you missed the talk at TOCC you missed a startling revelation of what people are capable of doing to hurt one another, and of small acts of kindness that can mean the difference between life and death.

She and her mother through grit and luck survived the Warsaw Ghetto and eventually emigrated to Israel, and in 1957 Wolosky visited the United States. She met her husband during that visit and has been here since.

Wolosky told the audience that she previously spoke to local high school students on the Nation and told them, "You should know about your own history because you have suffered too," alluding to the genocide and taking of land from Native Americans by settlers and the U.S. government. That exchange, Wolosky recalled, brought tears to two high school girls when they realized the parallel between her experience and what Native Americans were subject to 100 to 200 years ago.

O'odham woman sees parallel with woman's experience

Ofelia Rivas sat in the audience listening to Wanda Wolosky tell her story about growing up in the Warsaw Ghetto in 1940, and she heard the survivor say Native Americans in their history suffered a similar genocide. Rivas agreed. "An American Holocaust happened here when the Europeans arrived. But we are resilient," she said, noting that tribes must retain their languages and retain their histories to remember what has happened.

"I was moved by her history. There are so many things she said that moved me," Rivas said, especially the parallel made to American history regarding Native Americans.

"But what struck me the most was the extreme inhumanity of what she went through," Rivas said, "And she survived, she survived all of that. She was resilient."

Rivas noted that we can be somewhat thankful. On the "Nation we have some luck, we are still on our land, at least we have some of our land."

Story of survival is remarkable, but hard to relate to Karen Maldonado.

Karen Maldonado from Artesia Village saw a woman telling her story of surviving as a girl of five in the Warsaw Ghetto in 1940 during World War II.

She said though it was hard to relate to the atrocities the girl experienced, the story told by Wanda Wolosky was remarkable in its graphic details of death, hunger and survival during the German occupation of Poland.

"How do you go on to the next day, how do you survive? I don't know how I would have survived, I don't think I would have," Maldonado said, adding, "But she did. It was inspirational. She went through a lot and she is still here. She went through a war."

The Family 2018

The family: Lin, Sharon, Paul, and Chance

Sharon and Paul under the Navajo Talker statue at Window Rock

Granddaughter Jade, about to join the US Army

Granddaughter Lin

Afterword: The Fight For Statehood

After writing about the history of World War I, World War II, the Ghetto uprising and more, I would not feel fully satisfied if I did not write about Israel's struggle for independence from the British Mandate. Luckily for me I was able to meet some of the people who participated in the fight for statehood.

During World War II, Jews from Palestine volunteered for special intelligence and dangerous commando work for the British Army. The hope was, of course, that after the war Britain would help to establish a country for the Jews. But the Balfour Declaration was all but forgotten. British troops friendly to the Jewish cause were pulled out of Palestine to be replaced by new troops. These new troops did not know all of the contributions the Jews had made for the British, and treated the Jews no better than the Nazis.

Left with no choice, the Irgun Zvai Leumi was formed, a national military organization that was split from the Hagana.

The Irgun considered itself a force in the struggle for the survival of Palestine's Jewry and for the creation of the Jewish state. Their ideology was built on principles: the creation of a Jewish State and the existence of an armed Jewish force. Jews had the right to enter Palestine freely; all Jews devoted to the state had to be allied in the struggle for independence; any foreign power that supported the Jewish right for independence and statehood was an ally.

When they announced the struggle against the Palestine government, the Irgun stressed continued cooperation with the allied cause.

On November 6, 1944, Lord Moyne, the British Resident Minister in the Middle East, was shot in Cairo, Egypt. The two young assailants, once arrested, declared their membership in the "Fighters for the Freedom of Israel," and stated that the assassination was performed under orders. They further stated that they were sent to Cairo with the express purpose of murdering Lord Moyne. Their reason was that, as the head of the British Government in the Middle East's political department, he was closing the gates to the only place left for European Jewry, Palestine.

Their trial was held in Cairo, and their defense was good and very strong. They quoted the Balfour Declaration. The presiding judge leaned towards jail sentences, and Egypt's Prime Minister promised the Chief Rabbi of Cairo that Bet-Souri and Hakim would not be hanged. But Winston Churchill, the supposed "friend of the Jews," demanded that the two young men, just 24 and 18 years old, be hanged. Churchill wasn't just satisfied with the hanging; he demanded that all terrorist leaders be exposed (The Irgun Zvai Leumi, including young Jewish nationalists, were all prepared to lay down their lives for what they believed to be their just cause: a free Palestine, a country for the Jewish people. A Jewish kingdom).

Churchill went much further than this. He openly threatened liquidating Zionism if the Jews didn't liquidate these "gangsters" themselves. Instead of rejecting Churchill's statement, Zionist leaders bowed to the British blackmail and launched a violent campaign against the "national danger of terrorism." The Labor Federation, comprised of members of the Histadrut, pledged themselves to combat terrorism. A witch hunt began, with members of Irgun and the Stern group being kidnapped and handed over to British authorities. It was Jew against Jew just to please the "friend of the Jews."

The Irgun and Stern group warned the Jewish population against delivering Jewish patriots to the authorities . . . "for whom we are risking our lives and pouring our blood, if not to achieve indepenence in our homeland." This they repeated again and again. Hagana, a semi-official defense branch of the the Jewish Agency, began abducting members (mostly youths) of the Irgun and Stern group. They were detained and interrogated prior to being either released or held in protective custody. Information obtained was given to the police.

Many supporters of the official Zionist policy condemned the kidnappings. The Jewish Agency openly boasted about its cooperation with the administration in stamping out terrorism. Hundreds of Jews were rounded up daily and held without trial at the Latrun camp. Their arrests were based merely on suspicion. Hundreds were sent in chains on military transport aircraft to Eritrea (a country in the horn of Africa that borders Sudan in the west) without trial.

The British were determined that Palestine should never become a Jewish state. Europe's Jews were not the only problem; the basic aims of Israel's Fighters for Freedom were much more far reaching. The question of statehood was immediately brought to the world's attention. The assassination of Lord Moyne was an act that led in that direction.

My friend, Ester Rziel-Naor, joined her brother David in the Irgun. David was later killed by a German Luftwaffe bomb in Iraq when he was on a mission for the British. Ester became the first broadcaster in the Irgun's underground radio station, Kol Zion

Halohemet (Voice of Fighting Zion). She also wrote for the Irgun's newspaper and was a member of its command structure. When the British police raided Ester's parents' house in 1944 and found a radio transmitter, she and her husband were arrested. Her husband, Yehuda Naor, was taken to Acre prison and later deported to Africa, where he was jailed for over four years. Ester was released after serving seven month in the Bethlehem jail. She remained under house arrest and was constantly under investigation.

When the King David Hotel was bombed, Ester was arrested again and sent to the Latrun detention camp, where she was held for several weeks. After being released, she remained under strict surveillance.

When the state of Israel was established, Ester Rziel-Naor was elected to the Knesset, where she served for 25 years. Any time my husband and I went to Jerusalem we had an open invitation to visit her and listen to her and Yehuda's stories. Yehuda was very proud of his beautiful butterfly collection.

On Yom Kippur during the British Mandate, the Jews were given strict guidelines how they could pray at the Kotel (Western Wall). Prayer books, chairs, benches, all needed to be brought on that day and removed at conclusion of prayer. The blowing of the Shofar, made from a ram's horn, was strictly prohibit. (It was because this was a residential neighborhood and it would disturb the neighbors.) Interesting the call for the Muslim prayers, (the Muezzin) was alright, and no restriction on church bells. Only the sound of the Shofar was prohibited. Supposedly the British who governed Palestine did not wanted to antagonize the relationships with the other population. The Jews did not blow the Shofar on Rosh HaShanah (Jewish New Year), but on each Yom Kippur (Day of Atonement) between 1929 and 1947 you could heard the Shofar blowing, even though it was illegal, it was worth to take the risk. The Shofar blowers were teenage boys. They knew it was risky, and would lead to spending one night or six months in jail. They would hide the Shofar in their clothes. There were few blowers. If one was arrested, another could continue. The meaning of the Shofar sound is: I am allowed to be where I am and where I belong. To live in a place without restrictions and where our freedom is protected.

I write these things because the Jewish struggle is one that will continue. I was shocked to read what has occurred recently in Poland. The Polish president has just stated that the Poles should not be blamed for what the Germans did there during World War II. (It is illegal to accuse the Poles. Violations will be punished by fine or three years in jail.) Let's ask those who returned after surviving the war—from concentration camps and from hiding—only to be murdered by the Poles once they arrived. Of course, we can't ask them; they died before we could. Ask those who visit Poland with their families now, only wanting to show them where they lived before the war. What happens? When they knock on those doors just to show their families the homes, the Poles refuse to even open the doors. You can't change history.

After signing this new law into place, the Polish government has decided to make March 24th their Day of Remembrance to honor Poles who saved Jews during the Holocaust.

I have one thing I wish to say to the Polish president, and it's a direct quote from US Army General Anthony McAuliffe during World War II when the Germans suggested he surrender at Bastogne, France: "Nuts!"

Let's get one thing straight: even after all that occurred in the war, after all the struggles the Jews endured during and after the war just to gain their independence and have a country of their own, the Jewish struggle continues, and sometimes it feels as though the Holocaust means nothing to some non-Jews.

I wrote this book for many reasons, but mostly because I fervently hope that these sorts of atrocities—people killing other people only because they are somehow different—will eventually stop. When I speak to students, I remind them that the red blood that runs through all of our veins is the same. This is a powerful message, and it is one that I will continue to teach until I no longer can.

For many years this basket has been located in the Chase Bank on Esparanza Boulevard in Green Valley, AZ. Local residents use the basket to donate various small items for US troops deployed on dangerous missions overseas.

DEPARTMENT OF THE AIR FORCE
HEADQUARTERS 162D WING, (ANG)
1650 E PERIMETER WAY
TUCSON ARIZONA

02 April 2018

To whom it may concern:

    Wanda Wolosky, consistently donates personal care and hygiene items to the Family Readiness office at the 162nd Wing. These items are available for our local Airman and at times are shipped overseas to our deployed members. Wanda's support is greatly appreciated and we enjoy her as a 162nd community partner.

Respectfully,

Barb Gavre
Family Readiness Program Manager
162d Wing, AZANG
Barbara.d.gavre.civ@mail.mil
Office: 520-295-6566
Cell: 520-270-2241

This certificate is presented to

Wanda Wolosky

In recognition of Holocaust Remembrance 2018.

The Department of State, Western Passport Center would like to express our sincere appreciation for you taking the time out of your busy schedule to speak to us on the Holocaust Remembrance Day.

Awarded by
The Western Passport Center
April 12, 2018.

Carol L Aguilar

Carol Aguilar
Assistant Director
Western Passport Center

April 9, 2018
Fort Huachuca
The only civilian recognition
plaque is located on the path:
"On the Military Intelligence
Soldier Heritage Walkway."

Granddaughter Jade being sworn in to the U.S. Army.

June 14, 2018. Goodfellow AFB, San Angelo, Tx
From left: Lieutenants: Jordan, Richard, Jessica, Wanda, Gail, Christian and John Garrett.

After All:

At the beginning of this book, I spoke a bit about how I started to write the story of my life. Every time I used to speak – either at schools, universities, colleges or on military bases – I would be asked why I didn't write my story. The opportunity arose when a teacher from Rio Rico, Arizona, volunteered to help me gather my thoughts in writing. Her name is Sarah Wright, and I am deeply grateful to her.

Following the first edition of this book, I had several years to recall other items that I thought were critical to my story, and started this second edition in 2017. I wish to thank Richard Fenwick for helping me with this new edition. I am grateful to him as well.

I always want to remind people that during the Holocaust, six million Jews perished, to include one and a half million children. Five million other people perished as well. The numbers are higher, though the correct number is unknown.

Despite all of this, as I wrote in the first edition, it took me some time to decide on a title for this book. But I believe that, no matter the circumstances, life is beautiful.

• • •

Acknowledgements

In the chapter "Ancient wars" I wrote that Jerusalem should be officially recognized as the Capital of the State of Israel.

On May 15, 2018, the 45th President of the United States of America, Donald J. Trump, relocated the US embassy from Tel-Aviv to Jerusalem, recognizing it officially and internationally as the Capital of the State of Israel. Since then, more embassies are following suit. Thank you Mr. President for fulfilling the promise so many of your predecessors failed to fulfill.

Thank you to all those who helped me in one way or another. I especially wish to thank Richard Fenwick, who took all that I dished out and made all my changes with a smile on his face. I imagine every change I made had him grinding his teeth (though I won't pay for the dentist). By the way, Richard is a retired Master Sergeant in the US Air Force, where he served 22 years as a Russian translator. Thank you for your patience, Rick.

There are several others I wish to thank as well:

Barbra Quade
Lloyd Bierstaker
David L. Graizbord, Ph.D
Ken Miller
Sarah Wright

All historical research was conducted by the author. For sources, please see the Works Cited section.

Works Cited

Brave and Desperate: 60 Years Since Warsaw Ghetto Uprising, 2004.

Polish Uprising from: Wikipedia, the Free Encyclopedia

The Israel-Palestine Conflict: One Hundred Years of War, 2005. James Gelvin.

The Balfour Declaration: The Origins of the Arab-Israeli Conflict, 2010.

Muranowska 7: The Warsaw Ghetto Rising, 1966. Chaim Lazar

Flags over the Warsaw Ghetto, The Untold Story of the Warsaw Ghetto Uprising, 2011. Moshe Arens.

Photos: Reproductions from *Brave and Desperate*

Ilan Kfir, Danny Dor, Chava Biran, James Gelvin, Janathan Schneer

Parasailing in Hawaii with a friend

CPSIA information can be obtained
at www.ICGtesting.com
Printed in the USA
FSHW01n0940060918
51880FS